KU-184-020

Contents

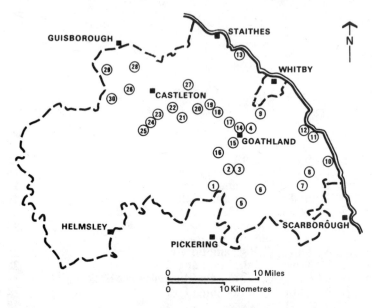

NORTH YORK MOORS NATIONAL PARK

── ── ── NATIONAL PARK BOUNDARY
NUMBERS DENOTE WALK START POINTS

GOING METRIC

The length of each walk in this book is given in miles and kilometres but within the text Imperial measurements are quoted. It is useful to bear the following approximations in mind:

$$5 \text{ miles} = 8 \text{ km}$$
$$\tfrac{1}{2} \text{ mile} = 800 \text{ metres}$$
$$1 \text{ metre} = 39 \text{ ins}$$

PLEASE LET US KNOW

Every care has been taken in the compilation of this book and the publishers cannot accept responsibility for any inaccuracies. But things change; paths are sometimes diverted; concrete bridges replace wooden ones; stiles disappear. Please let the publishers know if you discover anything like this on your way.

Foreword

Familiarity is commonly said to breed contempt! In the context of this book and my humble part in its creation, this old adage is surely confounded. The close and constant companionship of the author in traversing, with him, every inch of the way, has deepened my already high regard for his qualities—as a man and as a walker. That together we now know the terrain with a most detailed familiarity, loving it the more as we know it better, finally belies the saying.

Modestly claiming no professionalism in writing, Geoffrey White none the less shows that quality, because this harvested material has come from a well-informed and critical mind, presented with freshness, vivacity and justifiable confidence. This last can well be stressed to the reader, who may follow his guidance without any element of doubt or uncertainty.

If this work achieves nothing else, it sets into proper perspective the worth and joy of selective walking, be it on however small a scale. The uninitiated, no less than the experienced, should enjoy these adventures into otherwise unexplored country.

I commend to you this little book in the words of one with greater eloquence than I can hope to muster—John Milton:

'I shall detain you no longer in the demonstration of what we should not do, but strait conduct ye to a hillside, where I will point ye out the right path of a virtuous and noble education; laborious indeed at the first attempt, but else so smooth, so green, so full of goodly prospect, and melodious sounds on every side, that the harp of Orpheus was not more charming.

'In those vernal seasons of the year, when the air is calm and pleasant, it were an injury and sullenness against Nature not to go out and see her riches, and partake in her rejoicing with heaven and earth.'

GEOFFREY GREEN
Former President of the
Yorkshire Wayfarers

Introduction

The North York Moors National Park makes ideal walking country. It has a comparatively dry climate, wild, heather-covered moorland, gentle valleys, well kept villages, and clean fresh air—and it is accessible.

Few obstacles restrict the walker on the high moors, but the absence of walls and fences along the fast motor roads brings disaster to the farmer in the slaughter of sheep by careless motorists. Already the road out of Pickering towards Whitby has been partly fenced and who can blame the farmer for pressing for more fencing to protect his flocks? Please take your time in the car for the sake of the sheep.

As in my book *North York Moors Walks for Motorists* (*West and South*) I give a list of some good car parking places from which the newcomer to the National Park may like to take a stroll and a preliminary survey before embarking on some or all of the thirty circular walks which follow:

Gribdale Gate—Two miles east of Great Ayton—between Roseberry Topping and the Captain Cook monument.

Low Moor—Above the S-bend, three miles from Guisborough on the Whitby road.

Danby Beacon—Two miles from Danby.

Hob Hole—By the side of Baysdale Beck, between Kildale and Westerdale.

Ralph Crosses—Rosedale Head.

Lealholm—Free car park.

Glaisdale—By the river side near Beggar's Bridge.

Glaisdale Rigg—Three to four miles from Lealholm on the Rosedale road.

Hamer House—Two and a half miles from Rosedale Abbey on the Egton road.

Wheeldale Gill—Four miles south of Egton Bridge on the Stape road.

Grosmont—Free car park between the river Esk and the village.

Goathland—Free car park at north end of village.

Sleights—Top of Blue Bank.

Sil Howe—Two miles south of Blue Bank.

Eller Beck Bridge—Pickering/Whitby road near Fylingdales Early Warning Station.

Hole of Horcum—Pickering/Whitby road seven miles north of Pickering.

Levisham Station—Pickering/Whitby road, turn left four miles north of Pickering and continue through Lockton and Levisham.

Seive Dale and Snever Dale—Near Low Dalby on the Forest Drive north of Thornton Dale—a charge for the Forest Drive is made for the car.

High Staindale—Also on the Forest Drive.

Fylingthorpe—Four and a half miles south of Whitby on the Scarborough road, turn towards Fylingthorpe. High ground overlooking Robin Hood's Bay.

Falling Foss—One mile south of Littlebeck—reached from the B1416 road two miles south of Sneaton.

May Beck—Two miles south of Littlebeck—also reached from the B1416 road.

Reasty Bank—Near Swarth Howe, four miles north-east of Scalby.

Forge Valley—One and a half miles north of West Ayton.

Basin Howe—Overlooking Troutsdale two and a half miles north of Snainton.

Now try one of the thirty walks. The map for each walk is intended to be self-explanatory, but the reader is strongly recommended to obtain a copy of the Ordnance Survey Tourist map of the North York Moors which will add enormously to the pleasure and interest of the excursion.

An attempt has been made to offer a variety of walks, from wild moorland to gentle dale, and—a new dimension—the beautiful Yorkshire coast with its quaint, cliff-hanging villages of infinite charm. The coast path, as covered by the Cleveland Way, is good to walk upon in all parts; only samples have been taken for this book.

Here are my favourites (at the time of writing) of the rambles here described:

Moorland:	Walk 29
Moor and Dale:	Walks 2, 5 and 23
Forest:	Walk 7
Waterfalls:	Walks 9 and 14
Coast:	Walks 12 and 13

The *National Park Guide No. 4: North York Moors,* published by HMSO, is of great assistance and interest not only to those who wish to pursue hobbies in the National Park, but also to the walker who needs no further hobby to enhance his enjoyment. On the subject of access to land, I should like to quote from the Guide: 'Being easily accessible by road the National Park affords all-the-year-round exploration, but it is the walker or horseman who may best enjoy the intimacy of the Park for he may wander almost where he will. Access is remarkably free but, if in doubt, a polite enquiry will usually open all gates.' In spite of these encouraging words, *Walks for Motorists* has been written using only definitive rights of way, the well-trodden Lyke Wake Walk, or walks allowed by the Forestry Commission where entry is permitted to walkers but not to motorists.

The size of the area covered by this book gives scope for more walks than are suggested here—which themselves could be subject to variation according to the taste and energy of the reader, with the aid of the Ordnance Survey map. Attention is drawn to two bodies providing short but interesting walks in the Park: the Yorkshire Naturalists' Trust and the Forestry Commission whose addresses are given at the end of this book.

The Yorkshire Naturalists' Trust have Nature Reserves at:

	Grid Reference
Fen Bog	857982
Hayburn Wyke	006971
Ellerburn Bank	853850
Bridestones Nature Trail	872905
Hagg Wood Marsh	831893
Little Beck Wood	879049

The Forestry Commission's Forest Trails are:

Cropton Forest	—Newton Dale Trail	795943
Dalby Forest	—Sneverdale Trail, Low Dalby	856883
Langdale Forest	—Falling Foss Trail	889036
Langdale Forest	—Silpho Trail	965944
Wykeham Forest	—Wykeham Trail (three miles north of the village)	932883

Long distance walking is increasingly popular on the moors. For details see the list of useful publications, p96.

A leaflet issued by the National Park planning authority gives some useful advice to all who walk for pleasure across open moorland. You are recommended to obtain a copy and to follow its advice on the following subjects:

What clothing and equipment do I need?
How many in a party and how far?
Long Distance Walking;
Coastal Walks;
What can I do in an emergency?
If the weather turns bad?

Before you go leave information with someone at your base about your intended route and time of return.

The following advice I quote verbatim:

'*Unexploded shells* can still be found on the moors. For your own safety they must be left absolutely undisturbed. Please note the exact location, mark the spot with a few large stones and report the details to a local police station.

'*Adder Bite*. The moors are the home of the adder, the only poisonous snake in Britain. It is vital to keep the patient at rest and reassure him he will not die. A firm bandage (not too tight) may be applied on the heart side of the bite. Loosen this bandage for one minute every thirty minutes. Telephone the police: rescue will be arranged and the patient will be taken for hospital treatment.

'*Search and Rescue*. Thanks to the police and the North York Moors Rescue Teams, your personal safety on the moor is highly valued. Over the years, their services have been a welcome relief to those walkers who have been stranded on the moors.'

Much more information is given but in the meantime I would recommend the wearing of strong footwear (however short the journey I always prefer walking boots for the support they give to the ankles and for the grip on the ground); thick socks; waterproof, preferably an anorak or cagoule; and warm clothing. Carry, in addition to this guide, an Ordnance Survey Tourist map of the North York Moors and a compass, chiefly for interest but you may get lost; rucksack; some food, even if it is your intention to return for a meal; and first aid kit.

The Country Code

Enjoy the countryside and respect its life and work
Guard against all risk of fire
Fasten all gates
Keep your dogs under close control
Keep to public paths across farmland
Use gates and stiles to cross fences, hedges and walls
Leave livestock, crops and machinery alone
Take your litter home
Help to keep all water clean
Protect wildlife, plants and trees
Take special care on country roads
Make no unnecessary noise.

Walk 1

4 miles (6.5 km)

Rain Dale, Newton Dale and Stony Moor

If, in a wet season, you do not object to some muddy conditions this can be a rewarding walk, providing views of the tabular hills, some fine forestry country—especially in Rain Dale—a good opportunity for stepping out in Newton Dale, which is the very best example of a glacial meltwater cut, and finally through the heather on the aptly named Stony Moor.

There are several approaches to the chosen start point, below Rawcliff Bank, near Newton-on-Rawcliffe, but, if more convenient, the motorist could leave his car near Levisham station and cut into the circuit from there.

Assuming the Rawcliff start; if approaching from Kirbymoorside, turn off the Pickering road at Wrelton for Cawthorn, turn right towards Newton and after half a mile there is a track on the left, just beyond a wood, at which you might care to stop. The interest here is the famous Roman Camp which can be reached by walking half a mile down the track.

Resuming the motor ride, continue on the Newton road and, after taking a sharp left-hand turn, look out half a mile further on for a gap in the trees on the left and stop the car. There is a Forestry Commission sign here indicating this is Elleron View and it really is superb. Below is Elleron Lodge and the lake. Behind the lodge is Cropton Forest, which is the boundary between the area covered by this book and its predecessor, *North York Moors Walks for Motorists* (*West and South*). Further on can be seen Lastingham and the edges of the tabular hills. On a clear day the tip of Easterside Hill is visible over the general moorland skyline.

Resume the car journey in the direction of Newton but turn left towards Stape at the road junction. At the foot of Rawcliff Bank look out for the road at the beginning of the wood on the right, where a Forestry Commission sign reads 'No Admission to unauthorised vehicles'. Park the car here on the wide verge.

Motoring from Pickering, the road through Newton may be taken, but a better approach is *via* Lady Lumley's Grammar School. Three miles north of the turning from the school is a T junction. Turn left from here for half a mile if you intend to visit the Roman Camp, the track being on the right. But if the Camp is not in your programme, turn right for Elleron View and the Rawcliff parking point.

Before starting to walk away from the Stape road, it is worth noting that one and a half miles further north the tarred road gives way to a moorland road, good for walking on, leading to the

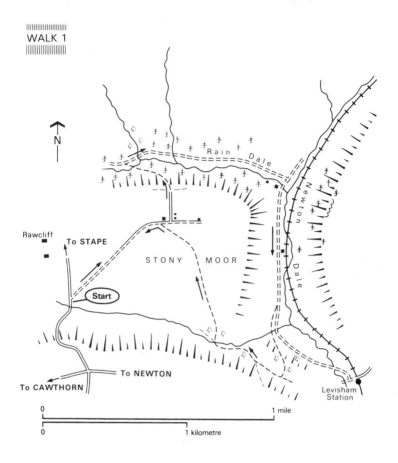

N

Rawcliff

To STAPE

STONY   MOOR

Start

To NEWTON

To CAWTHORN

Rain   Dale

Newton   Dale

Levisham
Station

0   1 mile

0   1 kilometre

well-known Roman road, Wade's Causeway. But a nearer approach
to the excavated road is from the north—see Walks 15 and 16.

Take the forest road prohibit d to motors. The Forestry Commission allows walkers on its roads and paths, provided they are careful
not to start fires. Soon a clearing is reached from which to the right
front is a good view of the wooded edge of the hills—Newton Banks.
The road passes through a gateway and you are quickly at a corner of
Stony Moor. Keeping to the track, pass the first of three small farms
on the left. Ahead can be seen Levisham Moor on the other side of
Newton Dale. Pass some gorse and immediately before reaching the
second cottage, now disused, turn left up a green lane, leaving Stony
Moor for the time being. There are some gorse bushes in the lane
which soon passes into a glade of old conifers. Keep to the track
going straight on which will soon bring you to the edge of the lovely

11

valley of Rain Dale which has been well tree-planted and, with its side ravines, makes a fine sight. The forest road at the bottom is our next objective.

The track goes steeply downhill to the left. It becomes a little muddy and there is more gorse to negotiate. But soon the forest road is reached, tarred for a little way on this section; turn right and go downhill where the road passes over two becks, the stream babbling on the right for the rest of the way downhill until one arrives at a road junction in the valley bottom. Turn right. This is Newton Dale, a grand steep-sided valley which was used by the railway engineers for probably the most scenic railway route in the whole country. The line fell into disuse after the Beeching axe fell, but, happily, it has been resuscitated by the enthusiasm of the North York Moors Railway Society which operates trains between Pickering and Grosmont.

Walk down Newton Dale with the railway line and the wide Pickering beck on your left. Immediately you pass former railway cottages, behind which is the site of Raindale Mill which was removed to the Castle Museum at York, where it is now in full working order and visited by thousands every year. Next The Grange is passed on the left, soon after which beck and road come close together. Ahead can be seen a road sign showing a sharp turn to the left but before reaching it look to the right for a muddy green track between tall hedges. Take it, or, to avoid the mud, join it further along the road before the bend. Step across a small stream, go through a gate, and uphill on a clear bridle track. The left hand of the alternatives is the cleaner and leads to the same place. This is quite an uphill pull between trees.

On emerging from the trees turn right on to tracks in the green field between woods and, at the far end, go through a gate into the upper wood and on to a wide but muddy track which joins one coming down from the left (from Newton). Turn right on to it and continue through the trees. Soon you are walking by the side of a stream which, after passing through a gap in a pole fence, you cross by stepping stones and climb up through a birch glade on to Stony Moor.

Go straight ahead on the track crossing the moor—a pleasant, heather-covered, rocky place. Looking across to the right over Newton Dale, you should see a square building on a shelf of land halfway up the other side. This is Skelton Tower. The track goes towards the three farms or cottages seen on the outward journey and eventually bears towards the left hand side one. Turn left here to return on the forest road back to the car.

Walk 2

5 miles (8 km)

Hole of Horcum and
Levisham Moor

This is a good, clean, dry walk, most of the route of which can be seen when you stand on the edge of the Hole of Horcum (where hang-gliders may often be seen), which is the start point for today. Sloping on the other side, down from the hairpin bend of the main road above Saltergate Inn, is a well-defined track to the bottom of the valley. One and a half miles lower down, turn to the right, and right again at Dundale pond and then there is a lovely walk back across Levisham Moor on an ancient track alongside earthworks, diverting for a superb view of Newton Dale, and back past Seavy Pond and along the top of the moor which can be seen above the other side of the Hole of Horcum.

The parking place is eight miles north of Pickering on the Pickering/Whitby road. Leave the car on the car park just above the steep decline to the famous Saltergate Inn. A word on the spelling of Saltergate: the natural inclination is to spell it 'Saltersgate' with an 's', this being as it is pronounced by many locally but, as most maps leave out the second 's', this is as it shall be in this book. More on this subject is on display within the inn itself. The name is derived from its position on the old salt route from Robin Hood's Bay, by which salt was carried inland from the sea. The ancient track on which we shall return today must surely have been used by some of the salt carriers.

Walk down the hill by the side of the main road as far as the hairpin bend and keep to the left of some white railings. The heather moors are ahead, below which is the depression of Newton Dale, containing the railway line, famous for its beautiful setting. Soon to the right will be seen the installations of the Fylingdales Early Warning System, not a pretty sight from here, although, from some angles, the three 'golf balls' can look quite beautiful.

Pass over a stile to the left of a gate a few yards from the road and turn immediately to the left, going downhill on the well defined sunken track which slopes on the side of the hill to the bottom of the Hole. The hillsides all round are bracken-covered and make a lovely sight on a late Autumn afternoon when lit by the setting sun. The track goes down to a gate on the other side of a trickle of a stream. There are rights of way on both sides of the beck but it is now proposed to go down the left bank; go over the gate and pass to the right of the buildings of Low Horcum. Follow the tractor trail into the dip and half-way up the other side, leaving it before it reaches the wood to join a green track which passes mid-way between the

13

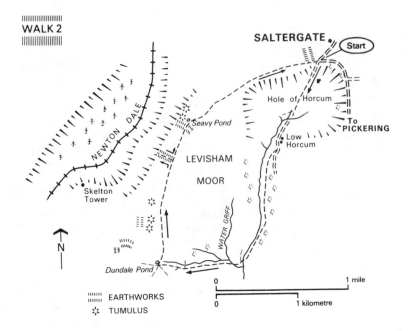

SALTERGATE

Start

Hole of Horcum

To PICKERING

Seavy Pond

Low Horcum

NEWTON DALE

LEVISHAM

MOOR

Skelton Tower

WATER GRIFF

N

Dundale Pond

||||||| EARTHWORKS
☆ TUMULUS

0   1 mile

0   1 kilometre

wood on the left and the stream on the right.

The field track eventually appears to lead to the woods but leave it after passing a group of three trees and go forward downhill to a track below the wood, nearly reaching the stream which is not much more than a trickle. Keep to the well-trodden single track as far as the right angle of a wall. Keep this on the left and go forward to a stile which pass over; continue, with the wall on your left, on the clear single track 20 to 40 feet above the stream until eventually it reaches the stream, crossing it on a footbridge.

(At this point, the track on the other side is very good; those who are just out for a stroll might care to return by it on the other side of the valley.)

But, to continue the whole of the suggested walk, go down stream for a few yards as far as a small beck coming in from the right. Turn up by the side of it and cross it just beyond a thorn tree. From here to the top of the moor, the stream is on the right, or rather, the stream bed, because usually the water course is dried up. The path is very clear and rises gently; ravines and old timber help to make a pleasant scene.

On leaving the trees the path rises to the left, but keep to the low ground, making towards the bushy topped tree ahead. Pass to the right of it and soon you are on cropped grass at the junction of five

14

The Hole of Horcum

tracks. Just beyond is Dundale Pond among reeds. Take a right-angled turn here to the right on to a very clear track going over the moor. The route can be seen a long way ahead, indicated by occasional concrete posts. So far, the green track has been through bracken but for the rest of the journey it is through heather.

Ancient earthworks and tumuli abound in these parts. 1,500 yards to the north of Dundale Pond, before reaching Seavy Pond, a high, bracken-covered mound goes away to the left through the heather. A diversion along it is recommended for about 300 yards where the earthwork ends at the edge of the moor. Here is one of the most dramatic views of Newton Dale with its railway snaking along the steep-sided, wooded valley. Halfway down on the left can be seen Skelton Tower which helps to fix one's position in relation to Walk 1.

Return to the main track and resume the journey, passing another—similar—long earthwork on the left and the little Seavy Pond. The wide trail continues over the moor, eventually skirting the top of the Hole of Horcum, known by many as the Devil's Punch-bowl. Legend has it that the devil, or perhaps a giant, scooped the soil and rock out of the moor to form the Hole of Horcum and dumped the debris a mile or so to the east to make Blakey Topping. The Romans are known to have used the Hole as an encampment.

The car will probably be seen on the other side and it will soon be reached.

This is a straightforward, dry walk which includes a scramble up the 300 feet or so of Blakey Topping, a fine sugar loaf outlier from the tabular hills which spread from Scarborough to Black Hambleton, all the way along the southern parts of the North York Moors. Other similar detached hills are Howden Hill to the east and Hawnby Hill and Easterside to the west, all, no doubt, detached by the action of springs over the centuries; all, no doubt, inviting to be climbed — because they are there, and because they are such good viewpoints. Unfortunately, not one boasts an official right of way footpath, but fortunately Blakey Topping is in the charge of the benevolent Forestry Commission which welcomes careful walkers.

The road from Pickering to Whitby meets the edge of the tabulars at Saltergate, famous for its views. Park the car, as in Walk No. 2, on the wide roadside stretch opposite the Hole of Horcum, near the eighth milestone. Take the track marked 'Footpath to Cross Cliff', tarred at this point. Go through a gate on which is printed 'Newgate Foot. Footpath only. No vehicles'. Continuing on the tarred road, soon you will see Blakey Topping.

On each side of the road is a big grassy expanse. Not very long ago the moors all around were heather-covered; to those who love wild places the change, due to ploughing and sowing, is for the worse. Away over to the left Hazelhead Moor still supported some heather on a recent visit; long may it remain.

Pass to the left of a new large building and to the right of a roadside row of young spruce trees on the straight road, slowly descending, then take the left fork on a partly concreted road going steeply down to the farm at Newgate Foot. Look left as you descend and note the track up the valley by the forest side, to which it is intended to return after climbing the Topping.

Pass the farm on a gravel road and observe on the left two corrugated asbestos huts beyond which is a black gate to which we shall return after the climb. In the meantime continue along the road, passing two old Nissen huts, as far as a cross track, at which point bear slightly left on a track through the bracken to the heather-covered top (the Topping). From here the first thing to be noticed will be the conglomerate installations of the Fylingdales Early Warning System, a blot on the landscape from this aspect. (However, there can be some beauty in the three radomes — the 'golf balls' — when the remaining buildings are masked and in certain lights — but that is when viewed from the other side.) Over to the east are the

16

young forests on Allerston High Moor, and to the south east the more mature Allerston Forest beyond the escarpment of Crosscliff Brow. Still further away to the east are the Bickley and Langdale Forests.

Retrace your steps to the black gate; go through into the field, joining a track over the small beck. Keep to the track, which partly crosses the valley. This is the track you could see before coming down to Newgate Foot; it goes up a lovely little valley, green between bracken and heather on one side, and forest with a background of the Topping on the other. At the other side of a gate is a fine double moorland track, among heather and bracken, leading gradually uphill to the head of the valley where Malo Cross stands — a stone in good condition on the parish boundary. This is one of the many crosses of ancient origin, some with a Christian background, some merely boundary stones, to be found on the moors. A competitive 53-mile walk was devised by the Scarborough Search and Rescue Team, the Crosses Walk, linking many of these stones, Malo Cross being one of them. Look back at Blakey Topping which is now end-on and appears to be almost conical.

Keep to this side of the stile and gate near here and turn left on a cart track through the heather, with a fence on your right. A steady

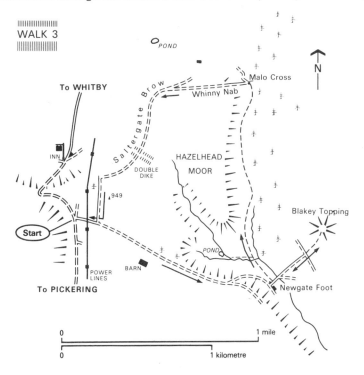

WALK 3

To WHITBY

POND

Malo Cross

Whinny Nab

N

Saltergate Brow

INN

HAZELHEAD

DOUBLE DIKE

MOOR

949

Blakey Topping

Start

POND

BARN

POWER LINES

Newgate Foot

To PICKERING

0   1 mile

0   1 kilometre

Blakey Topping

but gentle rise alongside Whinny Nab takes you up to Saltergate Brow. Down below is Nab Farm; the house seems to be in good repair but the outbuildings are derelict. Snaking across the moor is the Pickering/Whitby road, beyond which is the depression of Newton Dale.

Rejoin the grasslands on reaching the top, the path conforming to the shape of Saltergate Brow but gradually coming away from the edge after you have caught a sight of the inn below. Turn left at a conifer copse before reaching the power lines, passing to the right of a white triangulation pillar (height 949 feet). Join the side road at the first gate encountered on the outward journey and you will soon be back at the car.

Walk 4

8 miles (13 km)

Whinstone Ridge, Robin Hood's Bay Road, Lilla Howe and Foster Howes Rigg

A good walk, full of interest all the way, this one takes a lot of beating. In dry conditions, the ability to step out at a good pace, sniffing the ozone from the sea and the scents from the moor, examining the points of interest on the way, makes the distance seem much less than it really is, especially bearing in mind that most of the walking is on level ground.

The narrow ridge of volcanic rock, extensively quarried for its hard grey stone used for road making, extends from the North York Moors, through Teesdale at High Force, to the western isles of Scotland. The long quarries can be recognized where the molten rock was forced through narrow fissures. We are to follow the course of the ridge as far as the Robin Hood's Bay road at Blea Hill Beck. This ancient highway—now merely depressions in the heather moor—was once the route taken by traders in salt, and smugglers too, from Robin Hood's Bay to Saltergate, Pickering and beyond. We shall follow it as far as Lilla Howe, probably the oldest of all the ancient crosses on the moors; pause for views of the Lyke Wake route, the Fylingdales Early Warning System, part of the Derwent Valley, the forests and the coast beyond. The return will be on a good track past many old cairns.

Just south of the Goathland turning 6½ miles from Whitby on the Pickering road is a signpost 'Public Bridleway'. On the side of the road is good car parking near old whinstone quarries. Walk along the bridleway, where ahead can be seen a standing stone by the side of a forestry fence. Continue forward, keeping the fence on your left. Soon, the old track to Lilla bears to the right, but take the left fork which continues along the ridge to York Cross on a track well used by forestry vehicles. The cross, now only a stump, occupies a commanding position from which will be seen extensive afforestation and, on Pike Hill ahead, another line of old whinstone quarries. Tree planting has been intensive, but the foresters have left the line of the whinstone ridge almost undisturbed.

Pass the quarries on Pike Hill, go through a gate in the forest fence and cross Blea Hill Beck, picking up the track on the other side, on which turn right. This is the Robin Hood's Bay road, which is sometimes clear but sometimes offers alternative routes. When in doubt, keep to the right. The worst that could happen would be to reach the fence along the line marked 'Green Swang' which goes up to Louven Howe. In any case, you should see a signpost showing Saltergate to the left and Goathland to the right. From here Lilla Cross should be

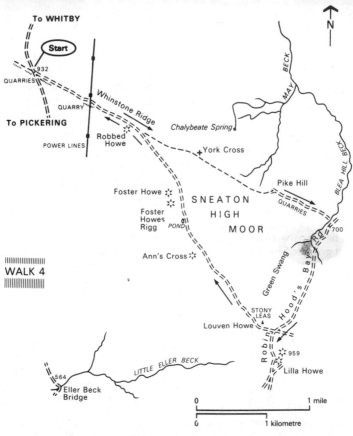

To WHITBY

Start

932

QUARRIES

To PICKERING

QUARRY

POWER LINES

Robbed Howe

Whinstone Ridge

Chalybeate Spring

York Cross

Foster Howe

Foster Howes Rigg

POND

Ann's Cross

WALK 4

SNEATON
HIGH
MOOR

Pike Hill

QUARRIES

700

Green Swang

Robin Hood's Bay Rd

STONY LEAS

Louven Howe

959

Lilla Howe

LITTLE ELLER BECK

564

Eller Beck
Bridge

MAY BECK

BLEA HILL BECK

N

0   1 mile

0   1 kilometre

seen on the way to Saltergate, well worth going to for the view.

The Lyke Wake Walk comes up from Eller Beck Bridge to the west and goes away to the east towards the radio mast, near Ravenscar, which should be seen in good weather. The Robin Hood's Bay road has been diverted to go outside the fence of the Fylingdales Early Warning System which looms ahead of you.

The way back is towards the signpost, previously visited, and on to Louven Howe which has several cairns and stones and a trig point. From here is a fine moorland track which passes, in turn on the left, Ann's Cross — an upright stone on a tumulus — a small pond, and the twin tumuli of Foster Howes. The main roads from Whitby — to Pickering on the left, and to Scarborough on the right — can be seen from here (or rather, the traffic on the roads) but they are sufficiently far away not to be disturbing. This is Foster Howes Rigg on Sneaton High Moor. To the left are acres of heather: to the right, newly planted forest.

When the Whinstone Ridge is joined, at Robbed Howe, there is a mile of walking on the track of the outward journey. The old quarries should be in sight all the time.

20

Walk 5   Stain Dale and the Bride Stones

6 or 2½ miles (9.5 or 4 km)

A visit to the Bride Stones is one of the highlights of walking on the North York Moors. These natural outcrops of hard-wearing siliceous sandstone and limestone have stood up to the weather, while the surrounding corrallian limestone has been worn away over the ages, leaving some fine shapes and climbable rocks, some free-standing, others small craggy cliffs.

The origin of the name is lost in obscurity but it has been advanced that the Stones were the scene of ancient marriage rites. The area is one of the few on the Moors owned by the National Trust; happily, it has thus been saved from the encroachment of the Forestry Commission. Nevertheless, that body has provided a good means of access — the Forest Drive from Dalby to Bickley, reached from Thornton Dale by taking the Whitby road and turning right after 1½ miles; or from the East, *via* Hackness and Langdale End, a charge being made for the car. Wild life must not be molested, nor fires lit, nor flowers picked at the Bride Stones because it is a nature reserve, maintained by the Yorkshire Naturalists Trust who, jointly with National Trust, established a three-mile nature walk here in 1973.

Thornton Dale (or Thornton-le-Dale) is one of England's most famously beautiful villages and must not be missed. The little hamlet of Ellerburn, upstream, is not so famous but has a quiet beauty of its own, with its cottage cafés by the stream. Here it was that Mrs Nelly Barnes lived — Aunty Nelly, as she was known to the visitors. She died early in 1971 but will long be remembered by ramblers and cyclists for her teas, conversation and lollipops given on departure. The road in the valley above Ellerburn is unsuitable for cars but the stream is the same as the one which will be crossed on the Forest Ride, reached from the road above the Dale.

Half a mile north of the forest village of Low Dalby is the Snever Dale car park. Continue north in the car to the next valley where, in Seive Dale, you may also park the car. The six mile route has been suggested in order to bring in a good walk along Stain Dale. If you wish to take advantage of this suggestion, stop at this car park — marked number 1 on the map overleaf. However, if you would prefer one of the shorter walks, continue driving on the Forest Drive for more than a mile and when you reach an 'S' bend from which you can see a farm on the other side of the valley, park the car beside the by-road on the right. Then walk down to the gate, bridge and Low Staindale Farm, which is the old Youth Hostel, and cut into the

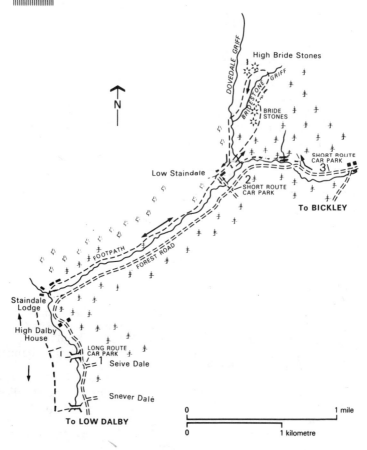

circuit as described below. This start point is marked No. 2 on the map.

Should there be no space left for your car at point 2, continue along the road for just over half a mile (point 3 on the map) where there is room for many cars. Here are toilets, a National Trust notice board and maps showing two walks, both well signposted, one being to the Bride Stones on a path through the wood giving direct access to the moor from which the Bride Stones will be seen and the circuit joined.

Those intending to walk six miles will see at Seive Dale a Forestry Commission notice about a Seive Dale round walk, 1½ miles (a blue

The Bride Stones

route), and Fox Hill round walk (a red route). It is the start of the red route we are to follow. Walk on the tarmac road, go down to a white footbridge, seen ahead. If you see some spotted sheep with four horns, they are Jacobs, from biblical times. At the bridge, red arrows point the way upstream. Soon another red arrow points uphill. Follow its direction to a track where still another red arrow points left, but leave the Fox Hill Forestry walk here and turn right, up-valley, on a green track. Soon the red roofs of Staindale Lodge will be seen ahead. The sound of a weir may be heard down on the right. Keep above the trees beyond the weir, cross a tarmac drive (to High Dalby House) and make for a small white gate leading to the garden of Staindale Lodge. On the right-of-way, pass to the front of the house on the gravel drive to a wide white gate. Pass to the right of two farm buildings; and cross a field, going towards a gate leading into a young plantation.

A wide track goes between the trees, from which some good views of Stain Dale are being increasingly obscured by the growing conifers, but, leaving the trees for a time, passing gorse bushes on the left with the stream below on the right, the view opens out. Keep to the track up the main valley. It gradually reaches stream level where there is a gate and a stile. Go over it; make up towards a wood ahead; pass through a gap in the fence. Soon Low Staindale comes into sight. (This was once a Youth Hostel).

Above and beyond the house you will see the bumps on the skyline — the Bride Stones. Pass through a gap in the fence just before reaching the house and join a track up the main valley behind the house. Step across a stream and go up to a gate leading into the wood ahead. Next to the gate is a notice indicating you are entering the Bride Stones Nature Reserve. Follow a clear path bearing left uphill through the woods. Below on the left is Dovedale Griff, along which we shall return.

On reaching the brow of the hill the jaded climber will be rewarded by the sight of the Bride Stones straight ahead; also, across the valley of Bridestones Griff, High Bride Stones. Unlike many of Brimham Rocks, these free-standing stones have not all been individually named. But one, a mushroom of a stone, is called the Pepperpot. 'Flat capped Paddy' could be an alternative name. (This may not seem obvious when near at hand, but when you eventually reach the bridge in the valley below, turn round and see whether you find the term descriptive.)

Take the left fork on the good path past the fifth stone, where the track will lead you below some outcrop rocks to cross Bridestone Griff and up the other side to the left of High Bride Stones. The intention is to go down the spur; but explore this other set of Stones first. Here are some cave formations and more craggy edges—useful for over-hang climbing practice.

The good path down the spur takes one to a wooden bridge over Dovedale Griff. Look back here for the sky-line view of the Bride Stones and see whether you agree with the suggested name for the mushroom stone.

The track keeps to the right of the stream until a hedge is reached. Keep to the right of it and you will join the outward trail about 150 yards above the stream crossing. Those who started from Car Park No. 3 could use stiles leading to a track just below the wood on the left which will lead them back to the car. Others, retrace the route back to the old Youth Hostel and turn left to cross the stream if the car was left at Park No. 2.

Longer route walkers continue down the valley on the right of the stream, which is the reverse of the outward journey route. You could, if you wish, vary the route beyond Staindale Lodge, on reaching the red arrow on the green track. Continue on the track, follow the arrows through the trees, which eventually lead you down to the white painted footbridge, Jubilee Bridge, across the Snever Dale car park and up the tarmac road to Seive Dale.

Walk 6   Langdale Rigg and Forest

5 miles (8 km)

The Forestry Commission has provided the walker with access to country not allowed to the motorist. Walking in the woods can sometimes be quite enjoyable, even though viewpoints may be few and far between. In the early days blanket planting was practised, but now there is some regard for the amenities.

One route the Commission has pioneered for the benefit of the walker is the Forest Walk from Reasty Bank, above Harwood Dale, to Allerston on the Scarborough/Thornton Dale road, giving a day's walk of 15½ miles, well marked with the sign of a man carrying a rucksack, blue on a white background. The route can be easily followed in either direction. In the opinion of the author, the best parts are in the north-east. Today we shall take a sample.

From all directions the motor ride to the start is magnificent. The road north from Snainton goes through lovely Troutsdale; from Scarborough either through East Ayton and Forge Valley or through Scalby and Hackness. From all these points pass the Moorcock Inn at Langdale End and drive to the left of the isolated Howden Hill, taking the first fork to the right — about half a mile beyond the Moorcock. If you approach the area from the Forest Drive through Bickley (see Walk 5), the fork is to the left just before reaching Howden Hill.

Park the car anywhere along this road. There is plenty of space by the roadside before going downhill to Hipperley Beck. Retrace your steps along the road until you are almost back to Howden Hill and within a quarter of a mile of the road junction. On the left are two gates side by side. Go through the first, indicated by a public footpath sign, uphill by the hedge side to the top of the field; keeping within the same field, turn left and make for the next hill — Langdale Rigg. Beyond the gate at the top right hand corner of the field turn immediately left on a good wide track going along the ridge. Below on your right is the gorge of the river Derwent, a meltwater cut from the glacial age, known as Lang Dale. Behind is a delightful view of the valley of the river Derwent as it makes its way towards another meltwater cut — the sylvan Forge Valley. Away on the left are the Bickley and Langdale Forests, beyond which is extensive moorland.

Coming to the top of the ridge you will find, alas, the moorland prepared for more tree planting (or the trees may already have been planted), so enjoy the views before they are obliterated. Ahead will be seen a gate to take you into a wide ride through well-established conifers, straight on for three-quarters of a mile; worth the walk for

WALK 6

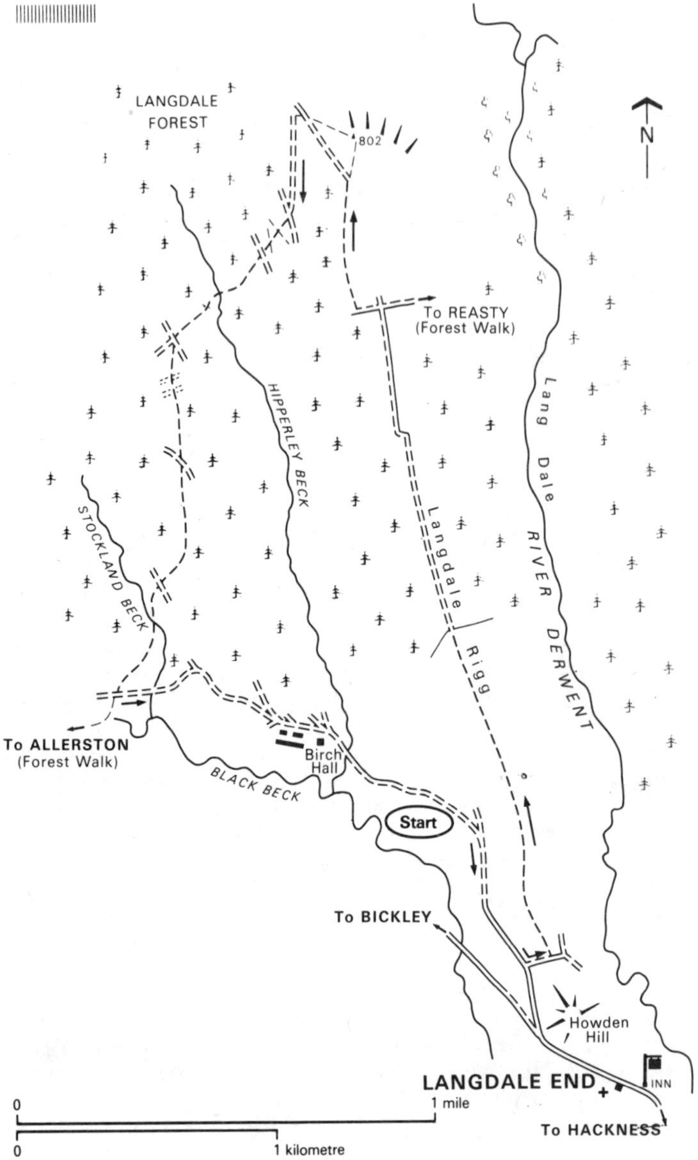

LANGDALE FOREST
802
N
To REASTY
(Forest Walk)
HIPPERLEY BECK
Langdale Rigg
Lang Dale
RIVER DERWENT
STOCKLAND BECK
To ALLERSTON
(Forest Walk)
Birch Hall
BLACK BECK
Start
To BICKLEY
Howden Hill
LANGDALE END
INN
To HACKNESS
0
1 mile
0
1 kilometre

the view to the north at the end. Here you know you have reached the Forest Walk because in front of you and to your left you see the blue man showing you the direction. To the right is Reasty Bank but turn to the left towards Allerston. For the next two miles the walker will be aided by this sign at every junction.

Soon the trail turns to the right towards the white triangulation pillar at Langdale Rigg End, 802 feet above sea level. It is worth visiting the trig point for a very fine view, a short departure from the trail which is rejoined near the foot of the first incline. Climb over a stile on the right to reach the view point. The valley in front is that of the Derwent in its early stages. Near its source on the left is Lilla Rigg. The moors in front of you are Lownorth Moor, Harwood Dale Moor and, on the horizon, Fylingdales Moor. To the north east, on a clear day, should be a sight of the old windmill near Ravenscar. Thus can be seen, from Lilla Howe along the horizon, to the windmill, the last weary eight miles of the Lyke Wake Walk.

From the trig point rejoin the trail below at a small gate almost opposite a left turn, suitably signed, which is the beginning of a footpath going in a south westerly direction for nearly two miles through nature's cathedral on a carpet of pine needles. All you have to do is to follow the signs until you reach a road 400 yards past Stockland Beck. But, for the record, here is a brief description of all sections up to that point: after 50 yards turn left; soon a forest road is reached; cross straight over and pass two junctions with rides; keep straight on. Go straight over another forest road. Cross Hipperley Beck by jumping or, if it has been restored, on a footbridge (missing when last visited). Cross a road junction and rejoin the path at the far side. Pass two fire breaks, the second stretching left and right from ridge to ridge. Reach an open viewpoint and bear to the right. Go over another ride. Rapidly downhill, continue forward until a forest road is crossed. Two hundred yards further on, you emerge from the trees at Stockland Beck, rippling through a most delightful valley in which to linger. Cross the beck on constructed stepping stones and follow the single track, between trees, to the metalled road. Leave the Forest Walk for today, turning left on the road. Bear right at an open triangle from which Bickley Forest can be seen on the other side of the valley. Now we are on the road which leads straight back to the car. As the first corner is turned the views ahead show Howden Hill and Langdale Rigg.

Green Forestry huts on the right are soon passed. Rides come in from the left. Birch Hall Farm is on the right followed by a descent on the road, now tarred, to the bridge over Hipperley Beck and the car beyond.

Walk 7

Whisper Dales and Lang Dale

Main Route: 7½ miles (12 km)
Option 1: 4½ miles (7 km)   Option 2: 7 miles (11 km)

The lovely valleys of Whisper Dales, Low Dales and High Dales (always referred to in the plural, probably because of their multiple heads) are quiet retreats amid the surrounding forests. The trees, usually above the 400 foot contour, add something to the shapes of the hills enclosing the green pastures and rippling streams. Today we shall take a sample; in addition, those who follow the whole of the suggested route will enjoy the delights of the river Derwent in the gorge of Lang Dale and the pastoral scene around Harwood Dale Beck, the site of the former Lownorth Camp, well known to many old soldiers and young cadets.

To reach the start point, which is the car park at the top of Reasty Bank at the north western end of the straight road on Suffield Moor, from Scarborough turn left in Scalby and from Whitby turn right off the Scarborough road at the Harwood Dale sign—but at the next junction keep straight on, climbing the bank sloping up to the trees at the top. The name Reasty is not shown on most maps, but the parking place is unmistakable, being the start of two trails: the Silpho Forest Trail, one of the nature trails for which Trail Guides are obtainable, often on the spot, for a few pence; and the Forest Walk to Allerston, 15½ miles. Both of these walks are recommended—but not today.

After enjoying the extensive views from Scarborough to Ravenscar, and Harwood Dale below, turn into the forest on a good track at a right angle to the cliff-edge Forest Walk (not to be taken today). Go straight across another track where a fox's head sign shows the direction of the nature trail on the right (but that, too, is not for us today). Soon the track forks. Take the lower one on the right and descend quite quickly through a gateway into open fields. The track goes down to the left of Whisperdales Farm to the stream. Cross a small beck but keep to the right bank of the main stream, on a good cart track which takes you across the stream less than half a mile lower down and keeps you on the left bank as far as Lowdales Farm. Before reaching the farm, when you come to a gate, look back for a general picture of the dale. The fine tree-covered hill dividing two of the valley heads has the quaint name of Hunter Noddle.

The track past the farm can be muddy. If you are not to take the first short cut the mud can be dodged by walking behind (to the left of) the farm buildings and through the field, where there is a right of way, to the left of the road. If you propose to take Option 1, your road is to the right immediately past the farm. The streams near this

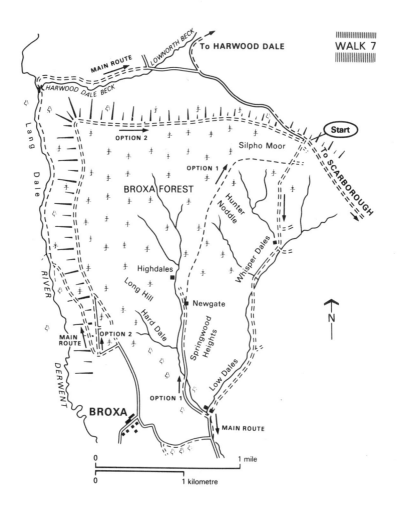

junction have been diverted into a culvert beneath the road for about 500 yards. Followers of Option 1 walk up the road, partly tarred, through a tree-covered valley which soon opens out, revealing High Dales — as beautiful as Whisper Dales. Immediately past the first house (Newgate) there is a good track on the right, signposted as a right of way. Take it for some better views (Highdales Farm is down on the left) and a forest walk back to the start.

Main walkers continue down Low Dales, either by field or by the road over the stream, until a bridge and ford are reached 500 yards away from the farm. The path turns off the road to the right and has become somewhat overgrown and muddy but the obstacles can be dodged and the path goes up through the wood to the north east corner of the hamlet of Broxa by way of a muddy lane. Turn right and keep on the road for half a mile and as soon as you arrive at Broxa Forest turn sharp left on a good footpath by the side of the trees. After a quarter of a mile there is a soft green ride on the right. Turn on to it for Option 2, which is the well defined route right back to the car park. The distance saved is only half a mile, but the going is good, the route level, and there are some fine views of moorland to the north from the last one-and-a-half mile stretch along the escarpment.

The main route is straight ahead on the track which soon turns downhill to the right, sloping in the same direction all the way through the trees to the river Derwent. Within a few yards of the junction of the path with the river bank, the Forest Walk is joined. To the left, over a substantial footbridge, is the way to Allerston. Straight on is back to Reasty, the northward path we are now to take by the side of the stream, sometimes rippling, sometimes gently flowing, always a delight to walk beside. After a mile of river side, under trees, the Forest Walk turns uphill and back to the cliff edge ride. Leave it here to continue beside the Derwent to its confluence with the water of Harwood Dale Beck (known as Lownorth Beck further upstream). A few steps more and a good metal footbridge spans the beck.

Cross it, turn right and pass some gorse bushes; go through a gate, turning right again. Keep the stream on your right; pass through a field where there are obvious signs of motor scrambling. If you seek peace avoid this area on summer Sundays. Reports are that loud-speaker announcements at this spot can be distinctly heard more than two miles away. Go through a small wood on a wide track and emerge on to the site of Lownorth Camp where the gorse is taking over but where there are concrete roads and old brick foundations.

Walk on the old roads or meander by the side of the stream until you reach a gate by a cattle grid and a sign which reads 'Footpath to Langdale End'. Turn to the right on a narrow public road and right again at the next junction. Soon you will be ascending the escarpment on the steep road leading to Reasty Top.

Walk 8

6½ miles (10.5 km)
Extended route 9½ miles (15 km)

Fylingdales Moor and Jugger Howe Beck

Fylingdales is one of the best known names on the North York Moors, chiefly because of the three 'golf balls' of the Early Warning System (not expected to be seen today). Old soldiers remember it as a bombing practice area. Occasionally, unexploded bombs are still found, walkers being warned not to touch any metal objects, but to carry out the drill mentioned in the introduction to this book. Others know it as part of the Lyke Wake Walk, the route now being established as passing from Lilla Howe, *via* Burn Howe and over Jugger Howe Beck. In the early days of the Walk, however, a number of alternative routes were offered, one being by Bloody Beck to Helwath Bridge. It is not true that the Beck was named by weary walkers; Bill Cowley, in his book *Lyke Wake Walk* tells us it was Bludebec in 1268.

The ravine of Jugger Howe Beck is pleasant country to walk in, but on 10 June 1972 the weather was atrocious. Continuous rain had filled the streams on the moors and the Beck had risen by about 10 feet, completely submerging the narrow footbridge. This coincided with one of the most popular weekends when hundreds of people were attempting the Walk, some being sponsored and anxious to support their cause. But although many dropped out, some managed to reach Jugger Howe Beck and were trapped. One man was quite exhausted; the Scarborough Search and Rescue Team were called out and had to bring in a helicopter to take the casualty to Scarborough Hospital. One of the Team, Malcolm Boyes, took some dramatic pictures which were published in the national press.

No doubt the reader will choose better conditions for today's walk. The extended route will take him to the exact scene of the rescue; the shorter route will lead him to the course the Rescue Team had to take.

Start from Chapel Farm 1½ miles down the side road from the Scarborough/Whitby road above Helwath Bridge. There are plenty of parking places by the roadside. A signpost just north of the farm shows 'Bridleway to Lilla'. Take this well-defined cart track and as you go down to the valley, observe on the left front the areas of Walks Nos 6 and 7, including Langdale Rigg End. The track curves to the right into woodland; keep to the main track until Jugger Howe Beck is reached. Cross a sleeper bridge, strong but in need of some repair when last visited, so take it gently. Go into scrubland and turn right, keeping near the right hand fence for less than a hundred yards, then

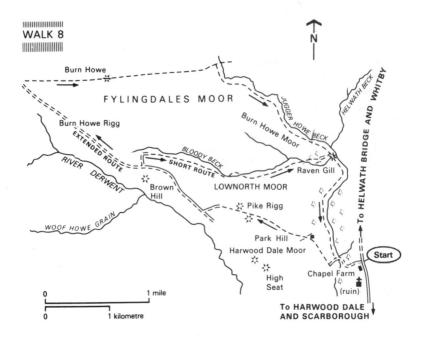

rejoin the cart road. Keep on this to the top of the hill, but note in the meantime a fence at the foot, which is the point of egress on return.

Go through the gate at the top and turn right, making towards the stone house, Park Hill, which you will soon see ahead. Follow a line of stumpy trees and pass to the left of Park Hill. Go through a small gate to a hard farm road, turn left and continue on this road heading towards farm buildings on the skyline. Join a hard cross track and turn right, continuing on this track until you see a gate ahead. As you approach this gate, bear left and, beyond an enclosure of conifers, you will find a small gate in the corner of the field. Pass through it and make your way uphill, with a wire fence on your right, to another gate at the top, leading to a dirt road between wire fences, wide apart.

Before turning to the right admire the view ahead, of the valley of the infant Derwent, with new forest country and white roads beyond. To the left is the gorge of Lang Dale into which the Derwent flows. On the right is a gate beside a cattle grid; go through or over, keeping to the dirt road. Now we are on Lownorth Moor on the Lilla Howe road. The green hill ahead is Brown Hill—the land all around has been recovered from virgin moor in recent years. On the immediate left front, the valley on the other side of the Derwent is Woof Howe Grain.

32

Keep the post and wire fence on your right until you have skirted Brown Hill, before reaching which the road peters out at a gate but continues beyond it as a green track, springy and good to walk upon. Go through another gate to the open heather moor, the turning point for those going on the shorter walk.

If you wish to join the main Lyke Wake route go straight on, using a good wide path through the heather, for another mile—which is one mile short of Lilla Cross—where you will see the unmistakable turning to the right marked by many Lyke Wake boots. Follow the track over Burn Howe to Jugger Howe Beck. At the lip of the moor, before the descent, decide whether or not to go down to the beck, not to cross it but to pick up a right of way on the right bank as far as Bloody Beck where the route described below will be joined. This route can, however, be very boggy and you may prefer to turn right at the moor edge, keeping to high ground until you are opposite Hellwath Beck, then descend to the right of way to the right bank of Jugger Howe Beck and on to the confluence with Bloody Beck at Raven Gill where the route described below will be joined either over stones at the junction or by the footbridge upstream.

Followers of the short cut will turn to the right, keeping to the left of the fence down to the infant Bloody Beck. Follow the fence round to the right, where the best going is above stream level, until you come to a cross fence. Descend to the stream, stride over it and a few yards further down re-cross it below a small waterfall and a good plunge—inviting on a hot day—returning to the fence side above and continuing downstream. A similar procedure is necessary several hundred yards further downstream at another cross fence, or you may decide now to keep to the left bank because this is where you should be when you reach the confluence of Bloody Beck with the stream from Burn Howe Moor. If you return to the fence side you have been following you have to come back to this stream junction at another cross fence. Having just passed the Burn Howe Beck climb up through the heather to a clear track along the edge of the ravine, which will take you to the top edge of a wood, soon going down below the cliffs into a glade of trees to cross the beck on an iron footbridge in Raven Gill.

From the bridge or stepping stones go straight forward on a green track through bracken on the right bank of Jugger Howe Beck. Here is a collapsed iron bridge but it is not the intention to cross the stream until we are almost home (and dry). Pass through a small iron gate and continue on the track, which is usually at stream level but here and there goes uphill through the birch trees to miss banks or bog but quickly returns to the side of the stream. This is a delightful part of the countryside and the path brings you back to the fence crossing seen on the outward journey.

Go into the lane and back to the sleeper bridge. Cross it, turn right on to the cart track again, and retrace your steps to the car.

Walk 9

Littlebeck and Falling Foss
Woodland Walk from Falling Foss
Woodland Walk from May Beck

Round trip: 6 miles (9.5 km)
3 miles (5 km) (Falling Foss)
4½ miles (7 km) (May Beck)

The two main features of today's walk are the delightful tiny hamlet of Littlebeck and the fine waterfall of Falling Foss, some 50 feet high, a mile upstream from the hamlet. The beckside walk between, through woodland noted for its flora from snowdrop to bramble, is a dry walk on good paths, with alternatives offered, usually on the right bank, sometimes on the left.

If nothing more is required, one of the two car parks reached from the Ruswarp/Scarborough road would make the best starting point. The Falling Foss car park has the added advantage of being the start of an official nature trail. Use of the May Beck car park adds mileage and forms a good centre for strolls upstream as well as down, including another attractive waterfall in Blea Hill Beck. The three mile and fo   and a half mile walks will not be described here as they are liberally indicated with finger posts. The farm trail, shown on an indicator board at the May Beck car park, is very popular.

The six mile journey gives the best approach to Littlebeck and a moorland walk in addition, but the last half mile at the head of Wash Beck can be marshy. About six miles from Whitby, and within sight of it, on the Pickering road (less than a mile south of the car park at the top of Blue Bank) there are two public bridleway signposts almost opposite each other. At the post on the east side of the road is a hard standing for several cars. Park here and walk towards Littlebeck on a green double track through heather, under the power lines, going steadily downhill towards the valley, joining a rough metalled road which leads down to a narrow lane between high banks, joins the Sleights road—a narrow tarred motor road—and continues forward downhill.

Sleights can be seen on the left, Aislaby beyond, on the other side of the Esk. Rounding a bend, the village comes into sight: trim houses built of the typical sandstone and pantiles of the North York Moors; a water mill; footbridges over the stream; old conifers in the valley bottom. Pass a chalet-type building housing a wood carver's workshop—a gnome is his trademark—and cross the beck on a footbridge. Pause at the gates to the Old Mill and Mill House (wooden gates bearing some fine carving, including the gnome); admire the fine buildings and trim grounds; go uphill for 30 yards to a seat and a Public Footpath sign.

Pass through a wicket-gate to a well-used path between hedges

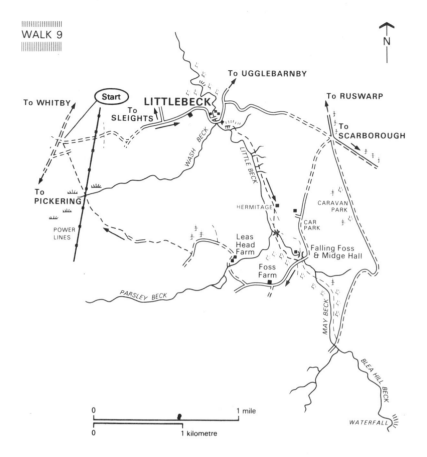

which soon passes into the woods. On the other side of the stream is a nature reserve of the Yorkshire Naturalists' Trust. The wide track climbs by the side of a waterfall in a feeder stream; at the top on the left, just out of sight, is a small pond which, when last visited, was alive with frogs. Sweep round to the right; ascend steps cut into a shale heap, from the top of which the main beck can be seen below in a sharp V which it has cut into the shale banks. The path bears left and descends almost to stream level for a short distance, then rises steadily until, nearly at the lip of the valley, it comes to an enormous rock hollowed out to make 'The Hermitage'; above the fine doorway is carved 'G.C. 1790'. It is said that this was the cell of a monk from Whitby who left the Abbey, seeking peace, at a time when it was inhabited by both monks and nuns.

Good views through the trees from the Hermitage include most of the route of our return journey.

35

The Hermitage

Take the lower of two tracks, continuing through the woods, signposted 'Forest Walk'. Cross the stream on a secure footbridge and keep to the main path, climbing upwards. Turn sharp left at stone steps with a protective fence, continuing uphill aided by frequent flights of stone steps. The path takes you to signposts, one indicating 'Short Trail' downhill, the other 'Long Trail' straight forward and over a rough road. Take the short trail downhill, descending to the beck, cross a footbridge, pass in front of Midge Hall, now boarded up, and go to the railings for a view of Falling Foss set in a hollowed-out rock among the trees.

Retrace your steps and go on to the rough road. If you wish to extend the walk you could take one of the footpaths on the left to May Beck car park, rejoining the described route at Foss Farm; otherwise, continue uphill on the firm dirt cart road, passing through two gates to the left of Foss Farm, now unoccupied, (the track goes through the farm yard), and into a lane between a hedge and a wire fence. Soon a recessed gateway is seen on the right; go through it on to a cart road, partly sunken, on the left hand side of a field. After going over the brow of a small hill you may catch a glimpse of a lake through trees on the left; soon you are crossing Parsley Beck on a concrete bridge, into the yard of Leas Head Farm and out of it through a gate on the left, taking a good farm road through one field.

Leave the field through a gate, where you should see a double signpost on the right showing a footpath ahead and a bridle road to the left. Take the bridle road, pass through one gate across it but at the next gate do not go through it but take a right-angled turn across the field, following exactly the direction of a bridleway signpost (which also shows we have been travelling towards Grosmont from the direction of Littlebeck). Once over the brow of the hill another bridleway signpost will be seen beside a gate. Follow its direction over rough ground through the next field to a gate taking you into a green lane between walls. Turn half right at the end, keeping to the left of a wall as far as the next gate. Pass through it on to the open moor.

Bear slightly right, walking between a ditch on the left and a wall on the right for about 100 yards, then bear left on a track leading from a gate towards pylons, making for a howe on the distant skyline. The grassy path between heather on the left and bracken on the right tends to lose itself here and there. The depression ahead is boggy but in order to avoid the worst of the bog, once the pylons have been passed, keep them roughly parallel on the right of your track through the heather. The car should be in sight and you should soon be home (and dry if you have remembered to bring a change of footwear).

Footnote: The holiday villages of Sleights and Grosmont are good walking centres, although in this volume no walks are started from them. Nevertheless, the circuits of Walks 9, 14, 15, 16 and 17 could easily be joined from either of these lovely places—perhaps in conjunction with a steam train journey from Grosmont or a scenic motor ride up Eskdale from Sleights.

Walks 18 and 19 could, however, be undertaken from Grosmont—adding four easy miles to the distance—by using the old toll road between Grosmont and Egton Bridge. This rough track along the valley gives fine views of the wooded country and, occasionally, of the Esk.

It is reached from the free car park in Grosmont (opposite the football field) on the Egton road by walking to the river and over the road bridge (but not the footbridge beyond) and taking the first turn on the left. It emerges past the Estate Office at Egton Bridge, near the Roman Catholic church—of noble dimensions. Turn left for both recommended start points.

2¾ miles (4.5 km)

Only the basic mileage has been shown because it is felt that people will want to wander at will, on the beach (no bathing on these rocky shores), on the cliffs north and south of the beck, and up the glen forming the central feature of the nature reserve. Here is a beauty spot which was particularly popular when the railway was running between Scarborough and Whitby, providing a scenic ride second only in grandeur to the Pickering/Whitby line. Today we shall walk to Hayburn Wyke along the Cleveland Way, signposted all along the cliffs as 'Coast Path', and return beside the disused line in pretty Newlands Dale.

The area surrounding the cove of Hayburn Wyke is a nature reserve in the charge of the Yorkshire Naturalists' Trust by arrangement with the Forestry Commission, Visitors are welcome free of charge but are requested not to pick flowers (which abound), uproot plants or in any way molest wild life. Fires may not be lit. Several waterfalls in the stream in the tree-covered valley contribute to the beauty of the scene, the most impressive being the fall gushing on to the beach itself.

The start of the walk is from Hood Lane, half a mile north of the village of Cloughton. Motor up the lane to the end (near Sycarham House) and park by the roadside. Walk on the rough cobbled road, left. From a seat half way along take a breather and a view of Cloughton Wyke, another stony cove, immediately below, and Scarborough in the middle distance. Pass a 'Public Footpath' sign and soon you will join the Coast Path.

The cliffs hereabouts are magnificent and the path is along the edge, going gradually uphill, soon to be protected by thorn bushes. Over the brow, Hayburn Wyke can be seen below with a wide sweep of moorland beyond; as the woodland is approached, the waterfall to the beach comes into sight. The ancient path beneath the feet is Rodger Trod, leading to a stile. Stone steps on the old path lead downwards through spruce trees and, later, deciduous trees of many kinds. Side tracks appear, but follow the direction of a 'Cleveland Way' sign, keeping to the main track going down hill. It is sometimes muddy, being sheltered from the sun and wind.

Before reaching the cross track on the valley floor there is a viewpoint from a rock at the edge of the trees. Here one may decide whether to take the simple journey now being described, or to wander for a while about the beach, along the cliffs (fifty wooden steps on the other side indicate what is in store there--but the flora on the south facing cliff make the climb worthwhile) or to explore upstream—or all of these things.

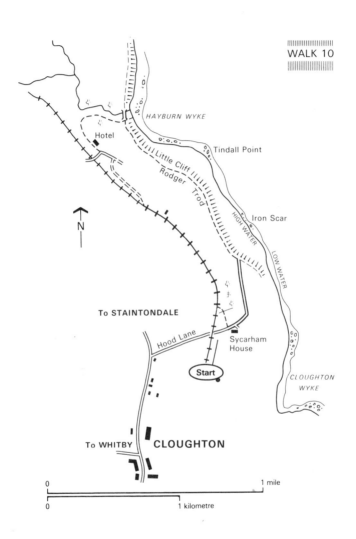

WALK 10

HAYBURN WYKE

Tindall Point

Hotel

Little Cliff

Rodger Trod

Iron Scar

N

HIGH WATER

LOW WATER

To STAINTONDALE

Hood Lane

Sycarham House

Start

CLOUGHTON WYKE

To WHITBY CLOUGHTON

0   1 mile

0   1 kilometre

It will take only a few minutes to reach the shore. Even if one is not to continue on the coast path, go to the substantial footbridge for the view upstream.

The main route back is along the path joined on reaching the valley bottom, the track being quite clear. Near the top of the ravine there is a side track to the right leading down to another good footbridge and a stream-side walk. If you wish, take it for a little return trip; if you miss the turning, you could pick up the track fifty yards further on where you reach a cross path at a Nature Reserve sign. Otherwise continue upwards until you come to a fork; bear right here; go over a stile; cross a field on a farm track bearing left; go over another stile by the side of a field gate into a farm yard; pass between the Hayburn Wyke Hotel and the private car park and take the lane on the left-hand side of the disused railway line, into a field. Bear right, keeping to the line side (not up the hill where the more prominent track goes). About 100 yards before reaching a cottage which can be seen ahead, get on to the railway track, which has been cleared and is well used. Keep to the track until the telegraph poles in Hood Lane can be seen, and leave it by a gate on the left to cross a narrow field to another gate and another small field, emerging near the car at a 'Public Footpath' sign.

Walk 11   Ravenscar and Stoupe Brow

4½ miles (7 km)

If to visit Stoupe Beck Sands add ¾ mile (1.0 km)

This is a simple walk combining moorland heather with the sight of the sea. On the outward journey there are fine views of the village of Robin Hood's Bay nestling in the cliff side: on the return, Ravenscar's high cliffs can be seen at their best. Ravenscar marks the end (or the beginning) of the Lyke Wake Walk. Ten thousand people complete this 40 mile moorland walk every year, so it is quite probable some will be around when you are in the area. You should be able to detect the finishers by their weariness, and, perhaps, stiffness!

Leave the car in the village by the roadside near the National Trust Information Centre (worth a visit) outside the grounds of the Raven Hall Hotel (built on the site of a Roman signal station) and take the track going slightly downhill back towards the old railway. (An alternative spot for parking is on the site of the old alum mine above the railway bridge near Stoupe Beck, reached from the crossroads at the top of the village.) From Ravenscar walk down the wide path to the old railway, now a cinder track, keeping it on your left as far as the bridge, which cross and walk up the lane, passing through a gate on the right into a field. The single track goes up beside a wall, a water tank, and through two gates to the left of a house reaching the tarred road above, on which turn right. It soon becomes a green road between wire fences.

The tumuli on the left, surmounted by a radio mast, are Beacon Howes. Over the brow of the hill the wide scene unfolds, one of the best views of the Bay. Down below are the railway track, Stoupe Beck and the cliff edge along which we shall return. Pass a cottage on the right and a peat stack on the left, the path narrowing to a single track along the line of telegraph poles before joining the tarred road from the crossroads at the top of the village. Note on the left the old quarries, where alum was extensively mined; on the right is the space for car parking alternatively suggested. Continue on the road over the railway bridge down to Stoupe Brow Cottage (more a farm than a cottage). Go forward past the car park at the end of the road and down to the beach on a distinct path through the trees.

If not to visit the sea shore turn right to the cliffs at a stile, marked 'Cleveland Way', and well signposted; it keeps to the cliff edge. At a stile a sign takes you uphill, with a fence and ditch on your left. At the next stile (on your left) turn left and proceed with a hedge-cum-fence on your right to a clear track and a field. Cross this

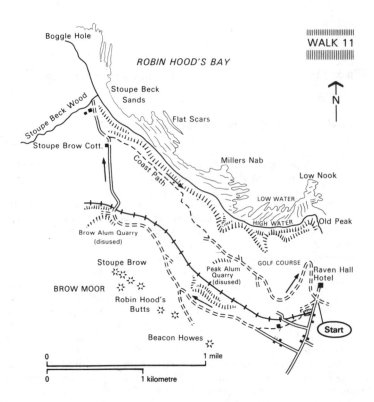

Boggle Hole

ROBIN HOOD'S BAY

N

Stoupe Beck
Sands

Stoupe Beck Wood

Flat Scars

Stoupe Brow Cott.

Coast Path

Millers Nab

Low Nook

LOW WATER

HIGH WATER

Old Peak

Brow Alum Quarry
(disused)

Stoupe Brow

GOLF COURSE

Raven Hall
Hotel

BROW MOOR

Peak Alum
Quarry
(disused)

Robin Hood's
Butts

Beacon Howes

Start

0   1 mile

0   1 kilometre

diagonally to a clear track over a stile. 500 yards further on, after
passing a National Trust sign you could continue to Ravenscar
as signposted or bear left where the track divides. The road can
be seen ahead winding its way towards the hotel. Soon the golf
course is on the left; the road takes a hairpin bend, turning inland
under the walls of the hotel grounds and emerging at the entrance
gate where there is a sign 'Public Footpath to the shore'.

Note*:* Walking on the track of the disused railway is allowed between
Scarborough and Whitby—useful to know if you wish to vary routes
or reduce gradients.

7 miles (11 km)

To exclude Stoupe Brow 6 miles (9.5 km)

The ancient fishing village of Robin Hood's Bay, clinging pictur-
esquely but precariously to the cliff side, has long been a holiday
resort for families who tend to revisit this place of beauty year after
year, often re-establishing holiday friendships with other families of
like mind. Sometimes included in the programme are joint walks to
such places as Falling Foss, Rigg Mill and even Goathland (with the
knowledge that one's dinner is being cooked in the communal
bakehouse) or, maybe in the evening, to Ramsdale, now to be
described—re-trodden by the author after more than fifty years and
giving him as much pleasure as in his boyhood.

Holiday visitors should cut into the route at Way Foot, where the
village road finishes at the beach, but the start point for the full walk
has been selected because (a) there is plenty of space for (free) car
parking and (b) the more strenuously minded may consider linking
this with Walk 11.

Motorists intending to leave the car at Stoupe Brow take the road
north west from the crossroads near the windmill at the top end of
Ravenscar and, after a little more than a mile, park the car by the
road side, below the old alum quarries, just before the road takes a
steep dip down to the old railway line.

Walk down the road which ends in a car park (not free) above the
beach and continue downhill on a track through the trees. If the tide
is out, the rest of the way to the village could be on the sands and
rocks of the beach, but if the cliff path is to be taken, cross the
concrete footbridge and take the right fork of the clay path to the
cliff top. Watch your step on this clay all along the cliff, especially if
there has been a shower of rain—also, be wary of overhanging parts
of the path. The stream under the concrete footbridge was Stoupe
Beck and the next is Mill Beck where the **Boggle Hole Youth Hostel** is
situated—additional buildings have been added to the old mill. If
not to go on the sands, cross the stream on a metal footbridge, taking
the right hand fork of the path up the cliff for the easier route to the
top (seats are provided for the weary).

The quaint romantic views of 'Bay'—the short name for the
village—come into sight after a wartime bunker is passed. Make use
of a series of wooden steps to bring you down to the 'front'.

Many nooks and crannies are there to be explored in the village
before returning to the slipway, known as Way Foot, near which is
Albion Street where a sign points 'To the cliffs'. Follow it, but do not

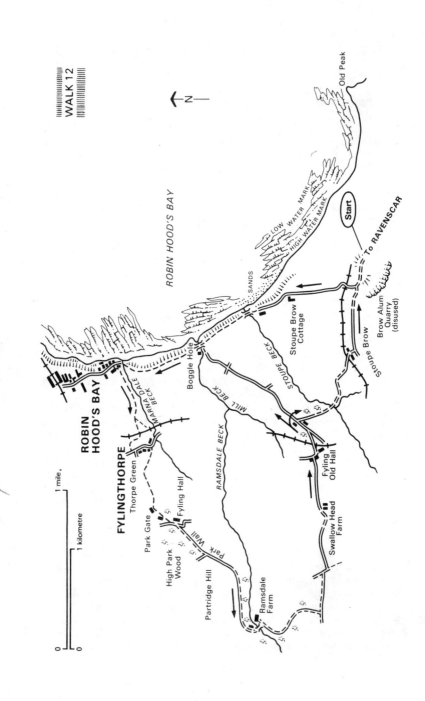

WALK 12

N

ROBIN HOOD'S BAY

ROBIN HOOD'S BAY

FYLINGTHORPE

Thorpe Green

Park Gate

Fyling Hall

High Park Wood

Park Wall

Partridge Hill

Ramsdale Farm

RAMSDALE BECK

Swallow Head Farm

Fyling Old Hall

MILL BECK

STOUPE BECK

Stoupe Brow Cottage

Stoupe Brow

Brow Alum Quarry (disused)

To RAVENSCAR

Start

SANDS

HIGH WATER MARK

LOW WATER MARK

Old Peak

Boggle Hole

MARNA DALE BECK

1 mile

1 kilometre

0

0

In Robin Hood's Bay

take the steps back to the cliff top; keep straight on, following the track which bends, keeping to the right hand side (left bank) of Marna Dale Beck on a distinct track through trees. Steps take one out of the dell to a stile and a clear field path from which Stoupe Brow can be seen on the left with Ravenscar beyond (Old Peak or South Cheek are old names for the headland). Ahead is High Park Wood on the side of Partridge Hill, our next objective.

Go through a gate, or over the stile by the side of it, and choose whether to bear left towards the farm at the other side of the old railway line or to keep straight on towards a camping field. Both routes lead to the tarmac road at the other side of the camp. Assuming the right hand path is taken, by the side of a hedge, climb two good stiles on to the railway track; turn right, walking for fifty yards to another stile on the left, which climb; turn half right to an oak tree and a stone stile; turn left on to a narrow path between wire fences to the houses; turn left on the road, going as far as Middlewood Crescent on the right. Walk to the end of it, bending right uphill. Go over a stile into a field and to another stile at the top corner; in the next field turn left up the hedge side on a little-used single track as far as a gate on the left, from which a diagonal track to the right will take you through two farm gates; turn left immediately, passing in front of cottages to a gate marked 'Public Footpath'; take an immediate right turn up some concrete steps to a partly paved trod, which is on the site of an ancient park wall, through the top corner of a wood; exit by a small white gate where a sign indicates we have come from the direction of Thorpe and Raw.

Turn left on the tarmac road but, just before reaching the fine residence, now a school, of Fyling Hall, take the upper of two side roads on the right, a straight, gravel, stone and sandy lane upwards through trees, continuing the line of the old park wall. From time to time, through the trees, there are views of the Bay and Ravenscar.

Bear left at the road junction, with trees now only on the left, which you leave altogether two hundred yards further on, giving a grand open view of Ramsdale. Pass a holiday bungalow and enter Oak Wood, still on the Wall road which eventually winds down to the fast-flowing Ramsdale Beck, crossed by a stone bridge. Downstream from the bridge is a waterfall by the side of the substantial, tall Ramsdale Mill, no longer in use as such.

Continue on the road, taking the hairpin bend past Ramsdale Farm, after which the track is grassy, though sometimes muddy, through fields, with the wood now on the right; pass through two gates, continuing on the track through woodland, emerging at a cross track, where turn left for Fyling Old Hall, as indicated by a finger post. The grass covered track comes to a gate on which is written 'Please keep to the road' but the only track on the other side is a single footpath through a field, keeping to the left of a stone wall as far as another stone wall across the line of march. Another signpost shows Fyling Old Hall to the right; follow its direction, passing through a gate into a lane.

Two bumps seen ahead, above the general line of the moor, are High Langdale End on the right and Broxa Forest on the left. The lane soon takes a left hand turn, and emerges into a field from which the track passes to the left of Swallow Head Farm. You may see black cattle hereabouts, with a white stripe round the middle — Belted Galloways, rather rare in these parts. The farm road, between hedges, leads to a tarmac road on which turn right for Fyling Old Hall in a lovely setting — a fine building.

Continue on the tarmac road; pass signs of the old railway; join another road; pass some houses with pretty gardens and roadside flowers; keep straight on if to return to Robin Hood's Bay by Boggle Hole, cliffs or sands.

If the car has been left on Stoupe Brow, turn to the right past the end house, 'White Lodge', on the road marked 'Unsuitable for motors'; this is a delightful green lane through woodlands, although it can be muddy near the Stoupe Beck crossing but improves on the other side. Keep to the main track which climbs up to the old railway track and passes to the left of the farm at Stoupe Brow; turn left at the moor road above the farm, passing through the former alum quarry back to the car.

Note: The railway track may be walked upon, if preferred.

Walk 13

10½ miles (17 km)
or simply Runswick Bay and Staithes 7 miles (11 km)

Kettleness, Runswick Bay and Staithes

A full day should be allowed for this walk, especially if Kettle Ness (the point), Runswick, and Staithes are to be explored and perhaps a bathe taken in Runswick Bay.

Because the walk is longer than most in this book, the reader may be tempted to cut out the Kettle Ness section, parking (for a fee) at either Runswick or Staithes. In doing this he would be missing some of the best views on the Yorkshire coast. On the other hand he would avoid a somewhat steep—and often slippery—slope into Hob Holes; the views from the cliffs at Kettleness could be saved for another day.

The full walk will now be described, the suggested points of entry for the shorter one being 'The Runswick Bay' inn at the top of the hill above the village or 'The Cod and Lobster' by the sea shore at Staithes. The return journey is by the same tracks as the outward one—except near the end; more use could have been made of the old railway track but right of way is on only part of it.

There is much to interest the visitor throughout the walk—massive evidence of the days of alum mining on the Ness, now very much an adventure playground; beautiful views of the holiday village of Runswick, with red-roofed, white or stone cottages clinging to the cliff side, subject alas to landslip—in fact, the whole of an earlier village collapsed into the sea in the seventeenth century; more signs of past industrial life at Port Mulgrave, from the old iron miners' cottages to the exit of the tunnel (now blocked) through which iron ore was passed down to the harbour; the fishing village of Staithes, quaint and full of romance of the old smuggling days; the women still wear their distinctive white bonnets on special occasions.

On the Whitby/Guisborough road, half a mile west of Lythe, a signpost pointing towards the sea shows Goldsborough to be 1¼ miles and Kettleness 2 miles away. Motor to Kettleness to the end of the tarmac at the cliff top where there is free parking for many cars.

The right of way is through the farm yard but it is worth going to the cliff edge for the view of Kettle Ness below, stark and awe-inspiring. To the left, the panorama of virtually the whole walk is before you, especially if you circle round the farm near the edge of the cliff. Three miles away is Old Nab, distinguished by the rock at the end, almost detached. Beyond are Boulby Cliffs at the other side of Staithes, 700 feet above the sea and the highest in Yorkshire. Immediately below are the flat 'paving' stones of the sea shore, a feature of the bays around here.

Rejoin the cliff path at the west gate of the farm yard, passing

47

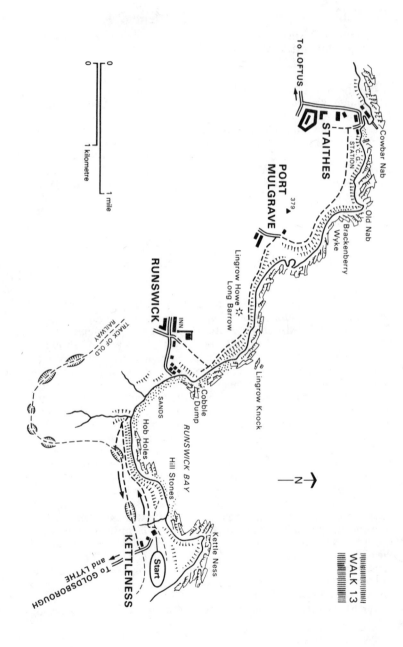

WALK 13

between the Coast Guard Rescue Station and a wooden bungalow. The path takes one round the head of the ravine and crosses the middle of two fields to regain the cliff top and, eventually, Hob Holes, first seen as a wild ravine with scrub and gorse. If conditions are damp, take care descending the clay path to the stream and the beach, sandy and suitable for bathing, preferably on return, towards the end of the day.

A walk across the sands, past the yacht club, brings one to Runswick village where the nooks and crannies among the charming houses and cottages are worthy of exploration if time permits. Artists and photographers need plenty of time to do justice to all the possibilities offered by this charming, quiet and sunny resort.

Since the collapse of the old road the only feasible way out is by the steep new road which goes straight up from the sea shore, past the car parks, to the pub at the cross roads — the 'Runswick Bay' — to the right of which are two notices denoting a public footpath. Keep to the left of the hedge and not the more obvious cinder track on the right, and to the right of a camping and caravanning field; climb over a stile, cross another field to a stile which brings you to the top of the cliff and, to the left, a straightforward cliff-edge walk as far as the little-used harbour of Port Mulgrave, now somewhat desolate but once a busy place for the despatch of iron ore.

Take a wide sweep round the bay to a stile, a cliff road and a row of houses with a peculiar perspective caused by a common sloping roof in conjunction with level stone walls. Pass the near end house and return to the cliff path. Soon there come into sight the buildings and chimneys of the potash mine below Boulby Cliffs.

At a stile where the outskirts of Staithes are first seen the path cuts across a field away from the cliff. Again, if time permits, one may be tempted to explore Old Nab, now seen on the right, another adventure playground, but one must return to this point because the cliffs between Old Nab and Staithes are dangerous and do not support a right of way. Brackenberry Wyke is another of those little bays with a flat rocky 'pavement' for a shore — good to look at but difficult to reach.

The path into Staithes passes through fields and by the side of a farm, into a narrow gully, joins another track by the side of a ravine, reaches houses and the church of St Peter the Fisherman, passes Captain Cook's cottage (he was a shop apprentice here before going to sea) and arrives at the sea front near the 'Cod and Lobster'. Note the way back before seeking quaintness or refreshment.

All that need be said about the return journey (apart from advising not to stray too far to the left) is a variation towards the end. At the top of the climb out of Hob Holes a single track across the field can be seen going towards a railway bridge. Take it and join the old railway track for a quick walk to the former Kettleness station, from which take a left turn on the tarmac road back to the start point on the cliff.

Walk 14   The Waterfalls of Goathland

Route 1: 3½ miles (5.5 km)
Route 2: 4¾ miles (7 km)
Route 3: 6 miles (9.5 km)

The waterfalls around Goathland are well known—in Eller Beck to the north and east of this fine moorland village, and in the gorge of West Beck, on the west side of the village. The most famous are Water Ark Foss, Thomason Foss, Mallyan Spout, and Nelly Ayre Foss. ('Force' is often used in place of 'Foss'). We shall visit two of these today, with a possible extension of our walk to a third on Route 3.

From the car park on the road to the railway station at the north east corner of the village, walk past the conveniences towards Darnholm and Beck Hole for about 70 yards; turn left off the road through a wicket gate by the side of a field gate into an enclosed footpath, with houses on the right and a small ravine on the left. We are walking on the site of the original railway—a steep slope down to Beck Hole; the line was diverted after a fatal accident in 1865. Leave the old railway site at the road, soon encountered; turn to the right, walking as far as the cross roads where turn left (towards Beck Hole); turn right just before the first house, into an enclosed footpath, following the direction of a signpost 'Public Footpath'. Go through a field between stiles, passing between old stone gateposts on a stone paved trod.

At the second stile you will see, below, the railway line winding its way through the gorge and you should hear the rushing water of Eller Beck. Steps cut into the steep slope go down to a strong footbridge over the water and beneath the railway bridge. The water passes through a narrow rock channel into a deep pool. Resist the temptation to jump the channel, being warned by the nearby gravestone of a sixteen-year-old boy who in 1908 was accidentally drowned.

Take the track climbing towards a seat at the top, but divert to the left for a good view of the waterfall near the second railway bridge. This is Water Ark Foss, falling 20 feet or so into the gorge where there are more drops, including Thomason Foss (not easily accessible) making a considerable fall in stream level. Now go up to the seat from which there is a good view of Water Ark Scar. Continue over the top on sheep-cropped grass, passing a hedge and a house on the left, and bracken on the right; pass below Hill House and downhill on the road, turning left over a railway bridge. Immediately below is the picturesque hamlet of Beck Hole. Take a footpath going down to the left; cross the road bridge over Eller Beck; pass, on the left, the Birch Hall Inn—a free house which also doubles as a shop—

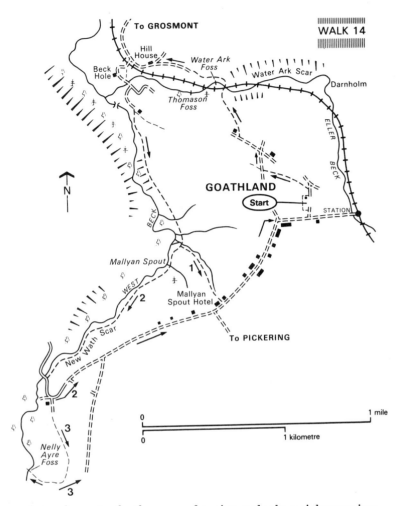

Hill House

Water Ark Foss

Beck Hole

Water Ark Scar

Darnholm

Thomason Foss

ELLER BECK

N

GOATHLAND

Start

STATION

BECK

Mallyan Spout

WEST

1

Mallyan Spout Hotel

2

New Wath Scar

To PICKERING

2

3

Nelly Ayre Foss

3

0   1 mile

0   1 kilometre

quaint and a centre for the game of quoits; and take a right turn just past it, through a gate into a green lane.

Pass through another gate on which is a notice 'Private. No access for vehicles. Public footpath and bridle path only'. Turn left and, opposite Incline Cottage, pass through a gate displaying a notice 'To the Mallyan'. (We are at the foot of the old railway incline.)

Now the path is beside West Beck at first; go over a stile; as soon as the woods are reached, the path starts to rise and keeps to the fence side to the top of the hill, although, to ease the gradient, one may take a zig-zag. The tree covered gorge is down on the right, deciduous trees on this side, mixed on the other — not only deciduous with conifers but the coniferous trees themselves are varied, thus avoiding monotony.

51

The uphill track continues above the trees until the houses of Goathland can be seen. Then the way descends steeply. Climb a stile; go over a little beck on a wooden footbridge; go steeply down — almost to water level; climb another stile; stride across another small stream on good solid stones. Now we have come to a very clear footpath through the trees by the side of the rippling West Beck again.

Soon you will reach a track coming in from the left. A bench marks the spot and up on the right there is a signpost: straight on 'Mallyan Spout', 'Goathland Village' to the left, and 'Beck Hole' from which we have come. Note this spot as the place of return for those electing to take Route One. But all continue forward for a very short distance, first on a wide path. Negotiate some rocks beneath steep cliffs. Suddenly, on the left, coming down from the cliff top, is Mallyan Spout. The height is impressive but the amount of water may disappoint, because it is only a small stream feeding West Beck.

Here a decision must be made whether to return and take the well trodden footpath back to the village — Route 1 — (which emerges at the Mallyan Spout Hotel) or whether to go on. The path ahead can be tricky, especially if the rocks are wet, but once the boulders, which can be seen ahead, have been passed the going is straightforward, if in places a little boggy, and there is a mile of lovely valley to come.

Assuming one has decided to continue upstream — on Route 2 — once past the rocks the path forks; keep left uphill but do not climb too far away from the beck. Returning to stream level some good pools for a plunge will be observed, but the best of all is a few hundred yards from the bridge where we shall emerge. Climb a stile; the valley opens out a little and the path through the trees is very clear. The cliffs on the left then close in at New Wath Scar and on the right the stream flows over some flat rocks. Eventually a large rock appears to dam the beck; below it is the plunge referred to earlier. The path takes a slightly upward track, soon reaching the road bridge. Turn left uphill as far as a sharp left hand turn in the road.

On Route 2 continue up the road, over a cattle grid, and straight on for Goathland. The scene emerging on the left shows the valley of the Murk Esk, the river formed by the merging of our two becks of today, the course of which can also be seen. Pass through the wide spaces of Goathland, sheep-cropped and green, back to the car park.

Route 3 walkers turn right at the sharp bend half-way up the hill from the bridge, going through an opening to the left of a two-storied house, continuing on a green track on the left hand side of a wall. Take the left fork before reaching fields, on a track which skirts the fields, emerging on open moor. Tracks lead down to Nelly Ayre Foss, a wide fall in West Beck. Return by the fence side and continue uphill to reach the Hunt House road, on which turn left, soon to join the Route 2 road, above the cattle grid, leading back to Goathland.

If Roman Road, Wade's Causeway, included 6 miles (9.5 km)

A pleasant section of the Lyke Wake Walk is over Howl Moor to Simon Howe from which there is a good general view of the Goathland area. Walking conditions are usually good on black, spongy peat. Today we shall join the Walk at Simon Howe after going along Two Howes Rigg on Goathland Moor; visit the stepping stones at Wheeldale Beck, a beauty spot and resting place for Lyke Wake walkers; and go up to Wade's Causeway, the excavated Roman road. Note, however, that this last item could be less strenuously incorporated into Walk 16, if preferred.

Park the car at the south end of Goathland, near the church. There is plenty of space for car parking on the village green, but to avoid annoying the residents it is advisable to keep away from the houses. Opposite the church is a house decorated with cart wheels. Go up the track to the right of it, past benches, and keep to the main green raised path not far from the road until, opposite the last house, it bears left. Two generations ago this was a golf course; pass an old green on the left and, among bracken and heather, a pond on the right.

When you reach two metal lengths on the ground, probably left behind by the Army and used for bridging, the track bears to the left, slightly away from the old sunken road, and makes for the Two Howes which can be seen ahead. These are two of the thousands of ancient burial mounds which can be found on the Moors, the first having a fine flat-topped stone cairn, the second supporting an equally good cairn, almost pointed.

From the first Howe take the single track towards Simon Howe which can now be seen on the sky line, a mile away, and rejoin the sunken route into which single tracks come and go. Make straight for Simon Howe through short heather which becomes patchy among grass and sphagnum moss, passing to the right of the white triangulation pillar on the way to the cairn. Here you will meet very clear tracks; to the left going towards the 'golf balls' of the Early Warning System; to the right down to Wheeldale. Ahead on the left is Whinny Nab (Walk 3) below which is the white Saltergate Inn. Further to the right, tree covered, is Wardle Rigg. Behind is a good view of the valley of the Murk Esk beyond Goathland.

Take the unmistakable track towards Wheeldale. The sheep on Howl Moor are typical of the ancient Black Face breed. The Two

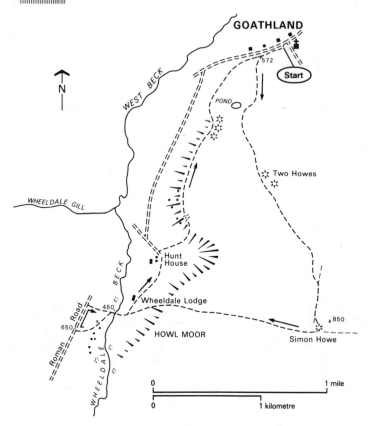

Howes, now on the right, look quite near, although they are a mile away. Suddenly, at the edge of the moor, Wheeldale is seen below. The first house is Wheeldale Lodge, now a Youth Hostel; beyond it is Hunt House and we shall pass both places on our way back. Immediately below is the track to the stepping stones, where you will probably want to linger awhile, after passing through a gate at the bottom of the track, where there is a notice reading 'Goathland Roman Road. Dogs must be kept on a lead'. Turn right for Wheeldale Lodge.

If, however, you have decided to visit the Roman road today (but see Walk 16), cross the very solid stepping stones and start climbing the steep bank. To go straight up would be to take the route of the Lyke Wake Walk, but after a few yards of ascent take the diagonal track on the left. Nearing the top, pass outcrops of large rocks from which have a look at the general view of Wheeldale; pass a sign reading: 'Roman Road. Horses must not be driven on Roman Road or verges. Ministry of Works.' Two hundred yards further on, past a sign showing the direction of the Youth Hostel back along our tracks, we arrive at the Roman road itself, excavated and rough, 17 feet wide. Another sign states that the road is the property of the Queen in right of her Duchy of Lancaster, with the Department of the Environment constituted Guardian of the monument. Turn right and walk as far as a stone hut, the headquarters of Geoff Hugill who maintains the road. He it was who told the writer that the moorland above the hut, which was being ploughed at the time, was not to be put down to forestry but converted to grassland.

Going up to the wall near the hut, it will be seen that the road has been excavated on the other side. But leave it here and go down by the wall side on the Lyke Wake route back to the stepping stones, which cross, and go back to the gate, turning left on a wide grassy track past the Youth Hostel and Hunt House to the tarred road which would lead you straight back to Goathland. You could avoid the local traffic, however, by taking a path over the moor, parallel to the road. To do this, walk uphill on the road from Hunt House, turning off on a tractor trail before reaching the first road junction.

The turn is sharp right, the trail leading through bracken to the heights above, reaching a stone cairn on the moor top. Make along the moor edge towards another cairn, from which keep above the bracken line on the edge of the heather, where various tracks lead to another cairn. Follow the double track below it for a short distance, but leave it when it turns towards the road below, keeping to an old green path which seems to be going up a small valley but which crosses the valley and keeps parallel with the road. From here there are views of the valley of West Beck which flows into the Murk Esk.

The sight of an old green makes one realise one has arrived back at the former golf course. Soon the outward track is re-joined near the point of departure from the road.

Walk 16   Wade's Causeway

3½ miles (5.5 km)

The course of the only Roman road to pass through north-east Yorkshire is not fully defined but on the North York Moors it is known to pass through Cawthorn Camp (see Walk 1), over Wheeldale and north to Whitby or Sandsend. On Wheeldale Moor a considerable stretch has been exposed, the excavations clearly showing the solid foundations. Today we shall walk alongside the part to the south of the road which may have been visited by those taking the extension of Walk 15, cross Wheeldale Beck on the famous stepping stones known to Lyke Wake walkers, return over Howl Moor and finish on forest rides at the ends of Gale Hill and Esp Riggs.

The starting point is near the water splash and footbridge where the tarmac ends on the Egton/Stape road, signposted also from Goathland, and it is more easily reached by car from the north. It could, however, be joined from the south but between Mauley Cross and the beginning of the walk the road is rough for 1¾ miles. Park the car on the moor beside the road immediately to the south of the ford.

Walk over the footbridge to the exposed Roman road and follow it uphill and cross the tarmac road. Go over a stile at a sign which reads 'Wheeldale Moor Roman Road. Part of a road connecting the Roman fort at Malton with the coast near Whitby, probably used in late Roman times as a link with the signal stations on that coast. The large stones now visible formed the raised central foundation and were originally covered by a finer road surface, probably of gravel. This monument is in the care of the Ministry of Public Buildings and Works'. As you walk by the side of the road you should see on the skyline ahead Two Howes and, to the right, Simon Howe, visited on Walk 15.

About 350 yards from a hut and wall ahead you should see another notice 'Wheeldale Moor Roman Road'. Turn right, down into the valley on a clear track. At some rock outcrops the Wheeldale Lodge Youth Hostel should be in sight. Just before reaching the stepping stones the Lyke Wake Walk is joined for a short time. Cross Wheeldale Beck, go through a gate, pass another Roman road signpost and go straight uphill on the well-trodden track. Near the hill crest, leave the Lyke Wake Walk and turn right on a clear double track through the heather, still going uphill but now gradually. Keep to the double track until you have crossed a small stream,

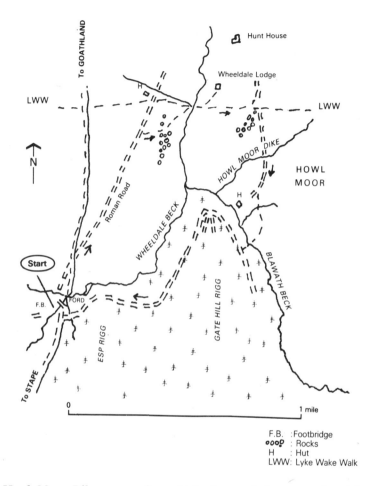

F.B. : Footbridge
ooo : Rocks
H : Hut
LWW: Lyke Wake Walk

Howl Moor Dike, soon after which the track bears to the right towards a Nissen hut and stone sheep shelter with a corrugated iron roof. But keep on high ground well to the left of the hut, looking for a stile into the forest about 350 yards from the hut. Step across Blawath Beck, a delightful stream, go over the stile and into the forest through a ride, soon to join a bigger ride.

Turn right on the main track. Soon two rides come in from the left but go forward downhill, now on gravel. Step out on this road for a mile, occasionally seeing Wheeldale moor through the trees. On leaving the forest through a gate you will be back where you started.

Walk 17   The Valley of the Murk Esk

5 miles (8 km)

7 miles (11 km) if starting from Goathland

The Murk Esk begins at the confluence of West Beck and Eller Beck at Beck Hole and ends where it joins the Esk at Grosmont (pronounced Gromont) two miles away as the crow flies. There can be few shorter rivers and few lovelier, winding as it does through woodlands and meadows, chosen by railway engineers for the line of the Whitby to Pickering railway, first in the valley bottom and, later, along the side (see Walk 14).

The walk will be described from Beck Hole but as car parking is somewhat limited there, the motorist may prefer to use facilities provided at Goathland, coming straight down the old incline from the car park (again, see Walk 14). For those approaching the area from the north, still another variation is to park the car by the side of the road between Grosmont and Egton Bridge on the south side of the river Esk, cutting into the walking circuit somewhere near South Side Farm.

At the elbow of the road at the bottom of the steep bank at Beck Hole a guide post indicates 'Public Footpath to Egton Bridge. Egton.' Pass through a gate on to this path between walls and very soon, reaching a similar notice, turn left as directed, noting that the path straight ahead (to Grosmont) is where one will emerge on the return journey.

Go through a gate on to the site of the old railway and turn right, passing over the river. Little more than 100 yards further on turn left at a fork in the path; go through a gate into a lane which crosses a stream three times on good footbridges. The third bridge is just beyond a ford; here rejoin the cart track going uphill, pass to the right of a ruined building and to the left of a house, Murk Side, higher up, curling to the right, behind it, on to a lane going slightly uphill, with good views down the valley.

The track goes to the left of Murk Side House where an uphill tarred road is joined but only as far as a sharp left hand turn where one goes straight forward over a stile and through a wood on a clear single track. Nearing the end of the wood the main path turns downhill but go straight on, over a stile into a field, which cross below a farm, Dowson Garth, making for the top end of a bit of wall in the hedge at the other side of the field. At this point cross a small stream on stones; go over the next field, making for the lower of two gates, top left, to get on to a farm track going away ahead. Keep on

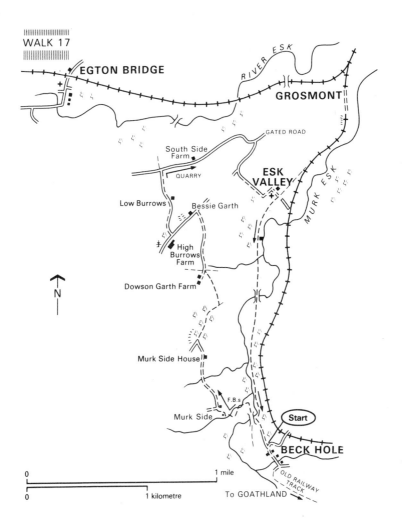

To GOATHLAND

this gated road as far as a tarred road, from which, looking right, Whitby and the sea should be in sight.

Turn left and pass a cottage named Bessie Garth on the right. In the field immediately past it is the site of a Roman camp. Only 300 yards of road walking is required before turning to the right at the beginning of a small wood opposite High Burrows Farm. A nice green track goes past Low Burrows to join the next tarred road at a gate by the side of a clump of holly trees. Now we are in Esk Dale and the water of the river Esk can be heard below. Egton Bridge, peaceful and serene, can be seen on the left; Egton is on the hill on

59

the other side of the valley; Grosmont is out of sight. Turn to the right and walk along the road (which is where the route could be joined by motorists from the north).

Turn right at the guide post to Esk Valley and take the next turn left downhill to the hamlet which is an isolated terrace of cottages — a reminder of the mining days in this area. Pass four disused cottages on the left and turn right after passing a 'phone box and the Methodist chapel. Here again is the site of the old railway; behind can be seen the junction of the old and the 'new'. The new line has recently been taken over and re-opened, after eight years of inaction, by the North York Moors Railway Company. It is, however, the course of the very old railway we are now to tread.

A gate and a stile are soon reached and our track goes alongside the Murk Esk. Pass an ingenious tree house; two former railway cottages with neat gardens: wild daffodils in season — quite a rival to Farndale — on to a footbridge where a railway bridge used to be.

Now the path is a lovely green lane, going into woodland almost camouflaging the old line. The river is on the right and soon can be seen the stonework on each side where there was a railway bridge. In 1933 there were terrible floods here when almost all the bridges were washed away. Climb over a short rise of ground and back to the side of the river, soon rejoining the outward track. Three hundred yards further on is Beck Hole.

Beck Hole Bridge

Walk 18   Egton Grange

4 miles (6.5 km)

In the little known valley of Egton Grange, so short as apparently not
to warrant the dignity of the name 'Dale', peace and quiet may easily
be found and the head of the dale reached with little effort.

The distance of the walk has been taken from the bridge over
Butter Beck. If the start is to be made from Egton Bridge village, add
another mile. Park the car by the side of the stream on the road to
Rosedale between the covered ford and the cottage on the other side
of the road, further south; walk over the bridge at the road junction
into an enclosed lane. Soon you are sufficiently high for views, to the
right, of the gorge of the river Esk, passing between the woods of
Limber Hill — of dramatic shape — and East Arncliff. Parts of the
big village of Glaisdale can be seen beyond the gorge.

Pass between Hall Grange Farmhouse and its buildings and continue on the farm road when soon you will see Grange Head, completely enclosed by Egton High Moor. Go through, and close behind
you, five metal gates, ingeniously secured. Woods are below on
the right; soon you are passing a plantation on the immediate
right and the fifth gate, followed by a cattle grid and open
ground.

The road takes a sharp right-hand turn to Grange Head Farm;
leave it here by going through a gate on the left. Follow an ancient
track, initially raised, and for less than a hundred yards almost back
tracking, but then turning uphill by the side of a ditch, the direction
being, generally, at right angles to the road along which you have
travelled. You will see an enclosed stake-and-wire pound on your
left, soon after which a fence will be reached where there are two
stone gateposts flanking the ditch. Go over the low wire, using the
stones provided, and, after continuing in the same direction for
about fifty yards, you will encounter a double track across your path.
The intention is to turn left here but it is worth going up to the
tumuli ahead for the view of Wheeldale and the moors above
Goathland and Grosmont. Whitby should also be seen and, away to
the right front, the Fylingdales Early Warning System with Whinny
Nab to the right of that.

The moorland track, green through heather, passes to the right of
the lower of a line of butts and joins the narrow metalled road (from
Egton to Stape) on which turn left and bear left at the fork, passing
between two standing stones. Pass through a gate, after which the
road is enclosed and soon descends, revealing views of Egton, Eskdale
and, to the right, Whitby Abbey.

Turn off the road at the first left turn, into a sandy lane, but leave it when it swings to the left towards Swang Farm, turning right into a leafy green lane. After a hundred yards you will see a farm building ahead and a gate across the track; another gate is on the left and this is the one to pass through on the right of way which goes down to Hall Grange Farm. Turn right in the lane at the farm—which is almost where you came in.

If this walk has been almost too gentle you could start straight away on Walk 19.

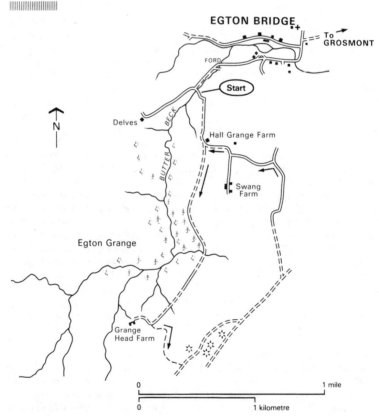

WALK 18

EGTON BRIDGE

To GROSMONT

FORD

Start

Delves

Hall Grange Farm

Swang Farm

Egton Grange

BUTTER BECK

N

Grange Head Farm

0   1 mile

0   1 kilometre

Walk 19
3 miles (5 km)

Beggar's Bridge and
East Arnecliff Wood

Although often muddy, this is a walk which should not be missed, taking in, as it does, some fine scenery of the river Esk passing through one of its most spectacular gorges caused chiefly by the meltwaters of the North Sea Glacier. The following quotation is taken from the *National Park Guide No 4: North York Moors*, published by HMSO. The words are by J.E. Hemingway: 'The effect of post-glacial diversion of the river is particularly distinctive in Lower Eskdale, where from the Lealholm moraine to the sea, the Esk has cut ten such gorges of varying depth, with the result that the valley floor is in the main useless for road construction.' This reference to roads pinpoints the difference between Eskdale and most other Yorkshire dales, which usually have a main road up the valley.

The tidy village of Egton Bridge, truly a holiday village—and famous for its Gooseberry Show held on the first or second Tuesday in August—is taken as the start point, but if you happen to be in the Glaisdale area you could park upstream from Beggar's Bridge where there is room between road and river, joining the walk there.

In Egton Bridge, opposite the Stape road end, near the Horse Shoe Hotel, a signpost shows the way to a public footpath to stepping stones. Follow it and cross the very solid stepping stones to an island and another series of stones to the other side of the river; up some steps and on to the hard road where you turn left towards Glaisdale. Walk beside the river. Pass through a wood; under the railway; pass Broom House Farm, continuing uphill for about a hundred yards. When the end of the wood on the left has been reached, go left through a field gate and walk along the top edge of the wood. Keeping to the track, cross the first stream at a cattle crossing or, to avoid mud, on a plank bridge a few yards downstream, and go through the middle of the next field, making for the dark patch of trees in the wood at the top of the next field where there is a stile into the wood.

A ride through the wood takes you to the right hand side of a hedge bordering a field. Keep close to the hedge and climb a stile at the far corner. Looking back from the stile, Egton can be seen on the hillside; Eskdale lies below.

Walk across the field; through the farm yard of Limber Hill Farm and, before turning left on the road, have a look over the hedge for a view of Eskdale winding to the right, Glaisdale village ahead, and the valley of Glaisdale to the left. The village was once an ironstone mining centre. In the mid-19th century there were three blast furnaces there.

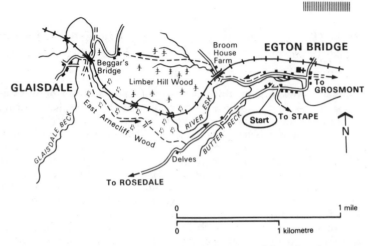

Go downhill on the road, bearing left on reaching the river, passing the aforementioned parking places by the attractive riverside. Beggar's Bridge is quickly reached—stone, seventeenth century and single span—a magnet for the artist, although modern road and railway bridges detract from the sylvan setting.

On the other side of the railway is a footbridge over Glaisdale Beck. Climb up the bank on the other side, entering East Arnecliff Wood (otherwise called Egton Wood) and turn left on a single path, initially following the river line, starting with a stepped path.

All the way through the woods the path is a clear one, often paved, known as the Packman's Trod. At first it is about a hundred feet above the river, then, at river level, where the water is calm, the track can be muddy. Ascending again, the path goes out of sight and sound of the Esk, but before reaching the top, you hear the sound of a weir; soon you will see it. A little later, at a high clearing, is the sight below of a fine Strid-like fall. This viewpoint is now obscured by trees.

Pass a rocky outcrop on the right, then over some mud where the walk is overlaid with timber. There are plenty of bilberries here. Soon the woodlands thin out for a little while and on the right there are high cliffs. Again, the sound of rushing water signals a fine stretch of white water below. A minute later you reach the Egton Bridge to Rosedale road at a signpost 'Footpath to Arnecliff Woods'.

Turn left, still within sight and sound of the river Esk on the left, through the trees. Coming to the valley bottom, the road goes alongside Butter Beck, a babbling brook. You may have parked the car here, remembering the place from Walk 18, or you may have to continue along the road into the village.

64

Walk 20   Lower Glaisdale

5½ miles (9 km)

The maps for Walks 20 and 21 are shown together, for the benefit of
walkers who would prefer to combine the two (cutting out the two
intermediate valley crossings). For the combined walk, if starting
from Glaisdale village (Beggar's Bridge or the railway station
nearby), follow Walk 20 in its early stages but keep on the hard road
as far as Wain Hill, then take the route of Walk 21 to Glaisdale Rigg,
rejoining Walk 20 where the track of the old railway joins the Rigg
road. This would be a 10 mile walk. The start point for Walk 21
could be used, if more convenient.

All that follows relates only to Walk 20.

Glaisdale is a scattered village, chiefly on the hillside at the
junction of the dale of the same name with Eskdale. There are signs
remaining of industrial activity of earlier centuries. Quoting from
the *National Park Guide No 4; North York Moors* (HMSO): 'Iron has
been made in Cleveland from mediaeval times. As early as 1207 the
family of Bolbec owned forges in Glaisdale, and when in 1223
Cleveland was granted to the Priory of Guisborough many
bloomeries for iron making were started. Peter de Brus gave to
Guisborough the iron ores in part of Glaisdale, and by 1271 there
were five small forges at work round Danby and two more in the
forest'. The scene is now completely pastoral, but added interest may
be found in the sturdily built cottages in the village, the shapes of old
weathered scars, and the green track of an old quarry railway, which
we shall use on the return journey.

West Arncliff Woods are not so accessible to the visitor as the
eastern sector (Walk 19) but they will be seen on the way.

From the railway arches near Beggar's Bridge — visit it if you have
not been there before (see Walk 19) — cross Glaisdale Beck over the
footbridge, keeping straight on past a notice reading 'Egton Woods'.
Soon the stone road begins to rise; take a left fork, pausing to admire
West Arncliff Woods, and keep on the track, now grassy, between
stone walls; pass Snowdon Nab Farm and turn right on the hard road
a little further on. Views to the left include Egton Grange, the valley
below (Walk 18), and on the sky line the ever present 'golf balls' of
the Early Warning System on Fylingdales Moor.

Thirty yards after crossing a cattle grid turn right on a very good
green moorland track through the heather and continue forward
alongside Bank House Brow Plantation. Go over a substantial stile
into the wood, taking a forward track sloping down through the
trees. Continue at the foot of the wood in a lane until you see a gate

in the wall on the right opposite a small stile; go through the gap on a track which soon slopes rapidly down to Bank House Farm. You will see West Arnecliff Woods now on your right. Go through the farm yard, cross a cattle grid on the road towards the next farm, New House, passing to the right of it to join the tarmac road, on which cross the valley floor, noting the shapes of the Arizona-like quarry workings on Glaisdale Rigg, ahead. Join the up-dale road at Witch Post Cottage and bear left, but after a few yards bear right on a road which initially is tarred but soon becomes a dirt track.

Go through a gate across the track, continuing forward until a small bridge over a gill can be seen ahead; before reaching the bridge, turn right towards the quarry, bearing left at a fork soon afterwards and passing to the left of the quarry, disused, deep, and now a dump, fortunately hidden from most eyes. The green track through the bracken is now on the site of the old railway, taking a straight course until it coincides with the Rigg road at an embankment before a cutting. Join the road and follow it down to The Green. Turn right on joining the motor road, passing the village hall and a row of stone cottages. Turn left at the Mitre Tavern and go steeply downhill, passing to the right of a fairly new road bridge over the river Esk. Rejoin the main road at Arnecliff Arms and turn left to complete the circuit.

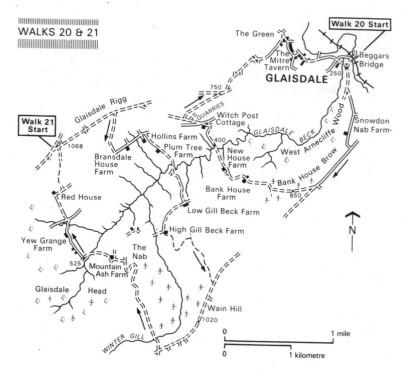

One of the joys of today's excursion is the motor ride to the start of the walk. If travelling from the south, the ride up Rosedale is itself a pleasure; climbing up to the high moors past the ruin of Hamer House — much used as a support point for Lyke Wake walkers — take the left turn at the signpost showing Glaisdale to be 6½ miles. After three miles of good but narrow road on Glaisdale Moor, passing the tumulus of Flat Howe on the left and views of Glaisdale and perhaps the sea on the right, look out for the white triangulation pillar, before which is a rough moorland road taking a right fork. Stop here and put your boots on.

Travellers from the north take the roads to Rosedale out of Houlsyke, Lealholm or Glaisdale which converge to ascend to Glaisdale Rigg, after giving fine views of Great Fryup Dale. The trig point will be recognised at the end of a long climb, on the left of the road. Go past it for the best parking on the left.

At 1068 feet above sea level take a look to the west at the craggy head of Great Fryup Dale and, through the gap of Fairy Cross plain (see Walk 22), there will be a glimpse of Little Fryup Dale. Away on the skyline, eleven miles to the north west, the tip of Roseberry Topping should be seen on a clear day. Before setting out, take a few steps in an easterly direction to the edge of the moor for a general view of the walk to come. Glaisdale Head will be seen on the right front; the farthest point of the walk will be the top tip of the conifer plantation of Wintergill on the other side of the dale.

Now step out on this fine walker's rough track among the heather on Glaisdale Rigg, signposted unfit for motor traffic — and may it always remain so! Soon it takes a downward turn and flattens out. Follow it for a thousand yards from the trig point and turn right (unless you intend to combine Walks 20 and 21). You will recognise the turning point, having passed a line of shooting butts on the left and a standing stone on which is marked 'Whitby Road'. Glaisdale Rigg is noted for its abundance of such stones. The track on the right is green and goes to the right of a stone wall, sloping backwards, and downwards.

Pass two thorn trees from which you will get a pretty comprehensive view of the broad head of the dale; looking back you will see the dale narrows as it approaches Eskdale. Go through a metal gate, after which the track becomes sunken, with gorse on each side. After passing through another gateway, turn left by the wall side through the field to the gate at the bottom.

Turn left on to the hard road, passing Bransdale House on the right. You will see two more farms downhill on the right, the nearer being Hollins Farm (which we shall miss), the further, Plum Tree (which we shall pass). So continue to the gateway on the right, labelled Plum Tree Farm; go over a cattle grid; pass through the farm yard, bearing left at the far end, through a gate and turn right on to a stone trod which is on the left hand side of a stone wall. Join the farm road, partly concreted, which bears right towards Glaisdale Beck; go over a very good footbridge comprising two huge stone slabs; continue forward through scrubland in the U-bend of the stream, taking the left hand gate ahead, where the cart track goes over a ditch; fifty yards further on go over a low climbable fence between gateposts, the hedge now being on your left until you pass through another gateway, when you then keep to the left of the hedge, walking towards Low Gill Beck Farm; turn to the right on the hard road which passes in front of the farm.

Walk up the dale on the tarred road to the next farm, High Gill Beck, suitably labelled, also advertising Bed and Breakfast. Turn left through the farm yard to the field gate beyond, which pass through and make for the small gate at the top left hand corner of the field, from which go straight up the hill, keeping the wall on your left; do not go through the first gate you see but continue to the next gateway in the top left hand corner of the wall; pass through and turn right — that is, continue in the direction you have been travelling — following the course of the right hand of two ditches coming down the moor, which, on reaching the moor top, passes between a stone cairn on the right and an upright stone on the left. The path becomes more distinct and takes you to the corner of Wintergill Plantation where you soon join the hard road linking Egton Bridge with Rosedale. Turn right.

As you walk along this minor motor road you will see ahead, on the skyline, the signs of the old coal pits at Hamer House on Rosedale Moor. The tumulus to the right of them, seen over the trees, is Flat Howe on Glaisdale Moor.

Three hundred yards past the end of the plantation, turn right on a green moorland track which soon passes over the infant Winter Gill and by the side of some wooden shooting butts. It is not long before the whole of Glaisdale comes into sight, including Glaisdale Head on the left, near which we shall pass. Starting to descend, go through a gate in a wall; now in a defile, join a single path through heather, making for a gap in the next wall, but instead of going through it, turn left on a track in a gully zig-zagging down to still another gap in another wall and Mountain Ash Farm straight down below it.

Join the road looping to the left of the farm, crossing the valley floor; cross the infant Glaisdale Beck; pass to the right of the private road to Midge Hall, two houses with lovely terraced gardens, and Yew Grange Farm, keeping to the hard road as far as the bridge over the babbling brook. The rough road back to the left is signposted to

Rosedale; go through the field gate near the junction and, uphill, keeping a wall on your right, make for a red-roofed building in a clump of trees on the skyline—this is Red House, now a ruin. At the top right hand corner of the field is a gate, not easily discernible from down below, and there is another gate a few yards away. Go through both and continue uphill, the wall now being on your left, until, at the top left hand corner of the field, you will see a gate on your right. Having turned right to go through it, go straight forward through bracken to join a good track left, leading away from a gate up a gully; cross a track going somewhat downhill away from Red House and continue sloping uphill. Sheep tracks bear to the right—follow them but keep climbing, joining a shallow gully where the track becomes more pronounced as it rounds the moor through bracken, bilberry and heather. Keep two upright stones away to your left.

In bright weather you should now see the sea north of Whitby, over to the right; soon, straight ahead, 1068 feet above its level, you should see the white triangulation pillar from which you set out earlier in the day.

Beggar's Bridge

Walk 22

Little Fryup Dale

7 miles (11.5 km)

Danby comprises several communities, the village to the north of the river Esk being known as Danby End, the part to the south being Ainthorpe, today's start point. On Danby Rigg, which we shall cross, there are more than eight hundred cairns, probably Bronze Age, and, on Danby High Moor, which we shall leave on our right, a settlement of ancient origin. Canon Atkinson was vicar here for 53 years; among other things he wrote *Forty years in a Moorland Parish*—a useful work of reference—published by Macmillan, London, in 1891.

After crossing the Rigg, the intention is to pass through the head of the romantic Little Fryup Dale; along the top on the other side, Heads; returning in Eskdale through Crag Wood and *via* Duck Bridge, an ancient monument.

Motoring, take the road in Ainthorpe signposted 'Fryup'; passing the Fox and Hounds and the triangular village green. Look out for roadside parking soon after starting to climb up the Rigg. Walking, pass two tennis courts at Bramble Carr and turn right off the road at a public bridleway signpost. You will find yourself on a green footpath, at first through gorse; through a gate, pass to the left of an old quarry, first through bracken, then heather. Pass three upright stones, the middle one being huge and strongly marked with weather channels and a big 'T'. Tumuli are all around. It is not long before you reach the lip of the moor and a fine view of Little Fryup Dale, with a glimpse of Great Fryup Dale through Fairy Cross Plain lying between the south end of Heads and the smooth pimple of Round Hill—left there, no doubt by the weather, because of its hard top.

The track slopes down towards Crossley House, joining the hard road at the bottom. Leave Crossley House on your right, continuing across the valley. Cross a cattle grid; pass some neat cottages and Stonebeck Gate Farm and when you have passed one field beyond the farm, go through a gate into a green lane on the left. At the next gate, turn immediately right along another green track between walls. Pass through a gate at the end, from which take a look at the heads of both Fryup Dales, for you are now in line with the dividing Round Hill, at a triangular conifer copse.

Turn left on a good track emerging from the conifers into the open moor, with a wall and green fields on the left. Pass another group of conifers, continuing forward but sloping up towards the top of Heads. When the path has reached its highest point it is clearly

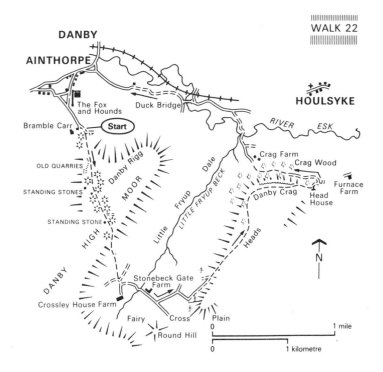

DANBY

AINTHORPE

HOULSYKE

The Fox
and Hounds
Duck Bridge

Bramble Carr

Start

RIVER ESK

OLD QUARRIES

Danby Rigg

MOOR

Crag Farm

Crag Wood

STANDING STONES

Little Fryup Dale

LITTLE FRYUP BECK

Furnace
Farm

Danby Crag

Head
House

STANDING STONE

HIGH

Heads

DANBY

N

Stonebeck Gate
Farm

Crossley House Farm

Fairy Cross Plain

Round Hill

0   1 mile

0   1 kilometre

defined along the edge of the escarpment, giving panoramic views of Little Fryup Dale, and goes all the way to a gate where wall meets trees.

Go through four field gates on a track which skirts the top of Danby Crag, as far as Head House. From here there are views over the trees of the neck of Little Fryup Dale and into Esk Dale. On the other side of the river Esk, the village of Houlsyke comes into sight and, behind it, Danby Beacon on Beacon Hill—a place worth visiting by the motorist since it gives grand all-round views from its height of 981 feet above sea level.

Approaching Head House Farm, a blue bridleway arrow will direct you to a gate to the left of the farm. At the other side, look down below. You will see a track beside a wall going towards Crag Wood on your left. The way down to this track may be very wet and you may prefer to keep to the wall side to the corner, before descending to take the track to the wood. Having taken a final view of Great Fryup Dale (on the right) go down to the track below, turn left and, with a wall on your right, go forward up Esk Dale and

71

Standing Stone on Danby Rigg
The pimple on the skyline is Roseberry Topping, 9 miles away

through a gate into Crag Wood on a green path through bracken. At the first fork go straight forward on the right hand track keeping on more or less level ground through this wood, a happy hunting ground for botanists. On emerging from the trees, Crag Farm will be seen on the right, but go straight forward, pass an isolated upright stone and go down into a lane which can be seen ahead; join the tarred farm road and cross the river Esk, wide upstream and downstream but narrow and rushing below the substantial bridge. Continue on this side road as far as the main dale road, on which turn left.

This is one of the few places in Esk Dale where there is a road going up and down the valley. Some ten thousand years ago the melting glacier waters formed Lake Eskdale where we are now walking. Lower down, the meltwater gorges make roadmaking difficult.

Seven hundred yards further on, the road forks; take the minor road straight on to Duck Bridge, a fine old bridge, steep and narrow. Below it, set in the fast flowing river, are stepping stones.

On the other side, turn to the right, finishing the walk back to Ainthorpe on this minor road. The railway is on the right, but, once the road is above its level, the views to the right towards Clitherbeck are attractive.

An alternative return from Duck Bridge would be to turn to the left, pass the remains of the old Danby Castle, turn right at the T junction—and you are on the road leading to the car.

The hub of the National Park is surely Rosedale Head, readily accessible to the motorist from north and south. Here are lots of landmarks, such as the Old Margery stone; crowds of crosses such as White Cross (or Fat Betty) and, most famous of all, Ralph Cross East with the hollow top for the leaving of alms for travellers (this author-traveller has not yet hit the jackpot); valuable viewpoints of Rosedale, Westerdale and Danby Dale; easy access to those dales, also to Farndale and, to the walker, Great and Little Fryup Dales. This general area is used for the start points for Walks 23, 24 and 25.

The scenery at the head of Great Fryup Dale is quite splendid, with crags and shapely hills, delightful becks and waterfalls, surrounded by heather moors.

One and a half miles on the road to Rosedale from Ralph Crosses at a junction with a by-road there is a signpost showing Castleton 6, Rosedale 3¼, Pickering 13. The signpost does not say where the by-road is going to, but it is to Little Fryup Dale. Take the side road — it is narrow (a notice warns you there are no passing places) but the surface is tarred — and leave the car at the first junction, with a rough moor road to the right, leading past Trough House, a stone shooting house which can be seen.

Walk along the rough road and when you have passed Trough House you will see signs of old pits on both sides. The track becomes a little damp as you round the head of the first of many streamlets feeding Great Fryup Beck. Pass a marker post at one of the streamlets and look left for a view of the shapely hills below the crag on the edge of the moor, known respectively as The Hills and The Scar. The head of Great Fryup Dale has quite an appearance of Lakeland. Continue on this track through heather, bilberry and bracken, noting a cairn which we shall rejoin on the return journey. Immediately beyond the cairn, but lower down on the left, is George Gap Spa, a chalybeate spring, of which there will be ample evidence on the return up the valley.

Continuing forward, the path keeps to the side of a dyke. When you get near a cairn on your right, look left for a view of Little Fryup Dale beyond Round Hill and Fairy Cross Plain. Climbing gently, one sees on the right a stone shooting butt and beyond, on Glaisdale Moor, a shooting house; the highest point is Peat Hill. The path is now a single track with another track a few feet away to the left, passing an upright stone. Keep alongside a ditch towards a foot-path sign on the Glaisdale Rigg Road (reading 'Bridleway to Trough House'). There is a good view of Glaisdale from here, also of the

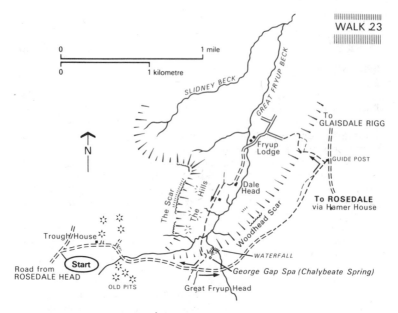

0   1 mile

0   1 kilometre

SLIDNEY BECK

GREAT FRYUP BECK

N

To
GLAISDALE RIGG

Fryup
Lodge

GUIDE POST

Dale
Head

The Scar

The Hills

Woodhead Scar

To ROSEDALE
via Hamer House

Trough House

Start

Road from
ROSEDALE HEAD

OLD PITS

WATERFALL

George Gap Spa (Chalybeate Spring)

Great Fryup Head

motor road on Glaisdale Rigg. Incidentally, this could be an alternative start point for the walk.

A faint track goes to the left at right angles to the road (it actually started some fifty yards back but it was worth coming to the finger post for the view); if it is difficult to find, make for the nab at the other side of Great Fryup Dale and Wood End Farm below it and you will soon pick up an ancient track curving down the hill-side to a wall. A holly tree by the side of the wall indicates the position of a gate which is out of sight. At the other side of the gate take a good look below at the route for most of the rest of the ramble.

Slope down right, through trees on a clear track, taking care on the steep part; at the bottom join a track through bracken, leftish, to a low gate at the beginning of a green lane; stride over the gate but beware the wire; go down the lane which is the official track but it can be wet in parts; turn left at the hard road at the bottom; pass through the yard of Fryup Lodge and go over Great Fryup Beck on a farm road bridge. Bear left on the farm track overlooking the lovely, tree-hung stream.

Here one has a better look at the east side of the valley, topped by Woodhead Scar, another fine bit of country. On reaching the buildings of Dale Head, now unoccupied, take the gate on the right. Immediately past the farm turn right, uphill, keeping a hedge on your left; step over the wire netting in the gateway at the top, where it is rather wet underfoot, but there are convenient stones. Turn left on a clear track going up the dale and at a fork in the path keep on

74

the higher track to rejoin the wall-side near a building. This is the region known as The Hills, well worth exploring if time permits, on the several tracks which go up and down and round about the bumps.

Resuming the walk and looking to the head of the valley one can see water splashing in a succession of falls, leaving a distinct deposit of iron. A free sample of spa water may be taken later on, for the track passes within a few yards of the fall. Go through a gate and down to the stream, which the path crosses on solid stones, another delightful spot, suitable for a lunch break. Climb up the bank on the other side and turn upwards, right, and then keep left on a clear path which crosses a gill and spirals over the next shoulder. Leave the path for a diversion to the waterfall for a taste of the waters — not too bad and it may do you good. You'll be feeling thirsty anyway after the sharp uphill climb. Just above the top fall you should find the chalybeate spring. Bear right to rejoin the outward track at the stone cairn.

Turn to the right for Trough House, which you should now be able to see, and as you reach the track junction from which you started the walk, you will probably find yourself voting it one of the best on the North York Moors.

Great Fryup Head

Walk 24

6 miles (9.5 km)

Danby High Moor and
Danby Botton

The Camphill Village Trust runs a centre for the mentally handicapped, occupying almost the whole of the head of Danby Dale in scattered communities. It provides a sheltered home environment for handicapped men and women able to hold jobs in open employment. Living together with the handicapped adult is important. In the village this takes the form of family households where houseparents, their own children and the handicapped share in common the daily routine of domestic life. No salaries or wages are paid either to the handicapped people or to any member of staff at the village. Whatever the work done, this is regarded as the individual's contribution to the expenses of the place.

One of the new long distance walks in the area is the Rosedale Circuit, organised by the Rambling Club Section of the Blackburn Welfare Society, British Aerospace, of Brough, Yorkshire, and the route passes close to Botton Hall, the hub of the community. The centre issues certificates to successful walkers on receipt of a voluntary donation and badges are issued by the Rosedale Circuit Secretary at British Aerospace. Today we shall see some of the country visited by the Rosedale Circuit walkers.

Start at the junction with the minor road, one and a half miles from Ralph Crosses where the signpost shows 'Rosedale 3¼, Pickering 13 and Castleton 6', where you would turn off for Trough House to do Walk 23. But this time leave the car at the main road junction unless it is your intention to combine the two walks, in which case the parking spot for Walk 23 would do just as well.

Walk along the minor tarred road on Danby High Moor for one and a half miles (or just over a mile from the alternative start). Soon you will see Danby Botton (Botton means a rounded valley) on the left and above it, on the skyline (if the weather is good) the tip of Roseberry Topping more than eleven miles away. Down dale is Castleton, the chief village of Upper Esk Dale (there is a bank there). Over to the left, on the other side of the valley, is Castleton Rigg on which you may see cars moving on the highway; the highest point on the Rigg is Brown Hill. When the Fryup Dales come into sight on the right, a few hundred yards before the road bends to the right, look for a shooting butt on the left, built on the site of the tumulus known as Wolf Pit. The butt is number five—painted on the inside. Take a track going away to the left to the edge of the moor.

Before descending the diagonal track to the right, have a look round. Most of the farms and newer buildings below belong to the

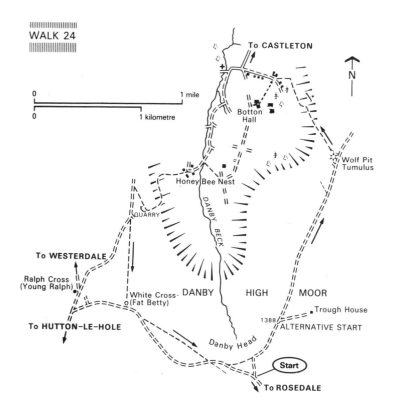

0 ⊢━━━━━━━━━━━━━━━━━━━━━⊣ 1 mile
0 ⊢━━━━━━━━━━━━━━━━━━━━━⊣ 1 kilometre

To CASTLETON

N

Botton Hall

Wolf Pit Tumulus

Honey Bee Nest

DANBY BECK

QUARRY

To WESTERDALE

Ralph Cross (Young Ralph)

White Cross (Fat Betty)

DANBY   HIGH   MOOR

To HUTTON-LE-HOLE

Trough House

1388 ALTERNATIVE START

Danby Head

Start

To ROSEDALE

Camphill Village Trust. The path goes below crags and to the top side of a wood, a hundred yards beyond which is a gate on the left. Go through it and downhill through the field to join a hard road at Botton Farm. Here you may choose between routes (a) or (b).

Route (a) Go straight down the road to the clear Danby Beck, taking the left turn, signposted 'Honeybeenest' (one word on the signpost). Keep to this quiet road through trees and meadows, ignoring side diversions, until, after crossing the main stream and passing two new buildings, one on each side, you go through Honeybeenest farmyard and pass through a gate.

Route (b) will be preferred by most, because it takes you through the most interesting Botton Village, as previously described. Just past 'The Cottage' on the left, turn left. On a gatepost is a notice 'Path to Village Centre'. Take this paved trod which goes to a café, post office, shops, including gift shop, and map of the village. Continue downhill a little until you reach the main road through the village. Turn left on the road, cross a wooden road bridge and keep

77

going on the tarmac road to cross tracks. Continue up the valley on a paved trod, go forward on a tarmac road signposted 'Honeybeenest farm area'. Cross a rough road to another paved trod which goes dowhill to join the Dale road on the valley floor. Turn left and pass through Honeybeenest Farm as described above. Go uphill by the side of a ditch, on the other side of which is a stone wall; beyond a gate at the top of the field turn sharply left on a track through bracken which soon rises gently. After four hundred yards on this path turn right by the side of a gully, continuing upwards until you reach an old quarry. The right of way turns acutely to the right below the quarry to meet the motor road 400 yards away; there then follows a sharp left turn to walk back another 400 yards to reach a point on the road, marked with upright posts, which can be seen from a quarry less than 300 yards away—and there is a track, not marked on the Ordnance Survey maps.

Having turned left on the Castleton Rigg road, towards Ralph Crosses which can be seen on the skyline, we shall walk on the road only as far as the white painted boundary stones, just past a low stone marked 'Danby Road' and 'Westerdale'. Westerdale Head can be seen on the right; the stream is Tower Beck soon becoming Whyett Beck which joins the river Esk a mile downstream from Westerdale village. At the head of the valley the Otter Hills are similar to 'The Hills' at the head of Great Fryup Dale.

Continuing in the line of march, you will notice the boundary stones are inscribed 'W' on the Westerdale Parish side and 'D' on the Danby Parish side. The path is a little vague at first but improves as you travel south. Soon after passing over the brow of the moor you will reach 'Fat Betty', a white boundary stone marked 'White Cross' on the OS maps. Now we shall follow the stones inscribed with an 'R' on the Rosedale side, but still a 'D' on the left.

Keep straight on, now on the motor road, passing to the left of one boundary stone. On the right is Rosedale Head; the Lion Inn on Blakey Ridge can be seen beyond. Take a track forward on the Left—made broad by ten thousand pairs of feet a year on the Lyke Wake Walk—passing more boundary stones. It can be boggy here in wet weather, so you could keep to the road if you prefer. The line of boundary stones crosses the road again, but now we shall leave this short stretch of the Lyke Wake Walk and continue on the road to the signpost where we started the walk. If, however, the car was parked at the alternative start point, take a faint track on the left, following the line of an ancient ditch, towards a notice board which is by the side of the minor road. Turn left on the road and you will soon see the car.

Walk 25

7½ miles (12 km)

Westerdale Moor and the Source of the Esk

Some parts of this route are boggy; in others, high heather must be negotiated. Boots should therefore be worn. The intention is to take the westerly Lyke Wake route from the Margery Bradley (or Old Margery) boundary stone above Blakey Rigg to the source of the Esk at Esklets; to go down Westerdale for less than a couple of miles; to go up the Nab and Howdale Hill on an ancient route, now little used; and to return to base *via* the disused ironstone Rosedale railway and Esklets again.

Old Margery will be found on the Castleton to Hutton-le-Hole road, half a mile south of Ralph Crosses. It is a tall, upright, weather-fluted rock, near which there is plenty of roadside parking. The chances are there will be Lyke Wake Walkers support cars waiting to welcome walkers near the half-way stage of their long journey.

Take the clear track going past shooting butts. As you reach the edge of this part of Westerdale Moor—High Hill Top—look across the valley and you should see a heap of lime which is beside the old mineral line and will form a good landmark on the return journey. Descending, dodge some boggy land as much as possible until, on the floor of the valley, the cropped grassy path through bracken is further indicated by a succession of white posts. Esklets Crag, on the right, is a typical feature of the dales leading northwards to the river Esk. The track crosses the infant river at a pleasant tree-strewn spot. White posts continue to mark the Lyke Wake route but today leave them after crossing the beck. We shall be returning to the Lyke Wake Walk later in the day.

Go toward heaps of stones, the demolished buildings of Esklets on the right, passing them on an obvious track. Pass through a gateway; cross a field to another gate, beyond which the path forks; take the right one going slightly downhill towards the stream. Go over a stile and a good concrete bridge over the water which is now the river Esk, the streamlets of Esklets having combined.

The path ascends a little, but generally keeps within earshot of the river. There are, in fact, two tracks going down the dale, the lower one being the correct right of way, but if you happen to be on the upper—and somewhat clearer—single track through the bracken make sure you join the lower one when you reach the copse opposite the Nab. Go over a stile, into a field, cutting off a loop in the stream, keeping to the left of a hedge; pass through a small wood, often muddy, reaching road, watersplash and footbridge over the Esk.

Walk uphill on the stone road which loops to the farm of High House. Go through the gate into the farm premises, then turn right through a wicket gate before the farmhouse. There is no path through the field but at the top right hand corner there are two gates in a re-entrant. Go through the gate straight ahead, at the foot of the Nab; turn right on an ancient track which rounds the Nab at roughly the same level as the gate, going into a gully on the White Gill side. If you pause as you emerge and look back, you should see two miles away the village of Westerdale among the trees.

Continuing round the Nab, White Gill—bracken covered—is on the right and to the front. Pass two large rocks in the gully where the track starts to rise and the gully bears left. Leave it here and go through rough heather, continuing slightly uphill and now facing Esklets. Bear right and make for the highest point, or slightly left of it, avoiding high heather as much as possible. Although we are on the right of way the track is difficult to find, but walking conditions improve as you go higher. As you round the top of the moor, Howdale Hill, you should observe to the left front the white heap of limestone previously mentioned. This landmark has been there for at least ten years, to the author's knowledge, and seems likely to remain. Eventually it is to be passed but, for easier walking along the railway track, it is just as well to continue forward until you hit the track. Turn left.

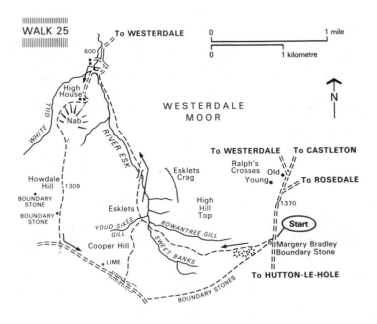

Esklets

The valley on the right is Farndale, the depression leading to it being Gill Beck where there is a waterfall referred to in the first book of this Series, *North York Moors Walks for Motorists* (*West and South*). In that book, also, more is said about the Rosedale railway, used in this section by Lyke Wake walkers for making up lost time.

Continue for about half a mile past the lime heap, where on the left there is a defaced notice which once read: 'Important. Please keep to footpaths indicated by white post signs. This route is shortest both to Westerdale Youth Hostel and for Lyke Wake Walk'. So turn to the left down the good track back to Esklets where the white posts will guide you first downhill, then uphill through the boggy ground and past the shooting butts to Old Margery.

The much easier path along the line of the boundary stones, leaving the railway track about a quarter of a mile further on, although well used, is not a right of way.

Walk 26   Baysdale

Less simple journey: 5½ miles (9 km)
Simple journey: 4¾ miles (7.5 km)

The beauty of this little known dale is its wildness and apparent inaccessibility by car, but when a corner is turned there will be seen dwellings and farms. The inhabitants reach the rest of the world not down the valley but over Battersby Moor to Kildale. I quote from the *National Park Guide No 4: North York Moors:* 'Baysdale. A lonely secluded valley near Battersby. Baysdale Abbey Farm is on the site of a Cistercian nunnery founded in the twelfth century. A small mediaeval ribbed bridge and a few sculptured stones are what remain from the early period, set in a beautiful situation.'

Today's walk will be up the valley on a walker's good moorland track, returning on the ancient Skinner Howe Cross Road, a single track the width of one's foot (sometimes only the width of the bottom of the furrows of a potato field) through the heather of the Hograh Moors. The distances shown do not include a visit to Baysdale Abbey, which would be but a simple extension along the valley road and back to the chosen route.

Park the car at Hob Hole, which lies in Baysdale on the narrow motor road between Kildale and Westerdale, a popular picnic place near a water splash and footbridge. There is plenty of room on the sheep-cropped turf. Walk up the hard road towards Kildale and turn left up the moorland track opposite the first road junction—a sandy, stony, grassy path through bracken and then through heather, on Kildale Moor. On the other side of the narrow dale are, in turn, Little Hograh Moor, Great Hograh Moor and Holiday Hill, more shapely than the other two. As the track bears leftwards, Shepherd's House will be seen beyond a well-established conifer wood. Later, those on the Simple Journey will pass it and take the track which can now be seen above the wood, half way up Holiday Hill. Those on the Less Simple Journey will go over the top.

The track bends past a farm building; goes downhill the length of a field, where, at some dilapidated farm buildings it turns right, descending into delightful country, nearly at stream level. There are gates to open and close before the track—now a farm road—crosses Baysdale Beck on a wooden bridge, after which pass through two more gates in quick succession to reach the narrow, tarmacadamed, Dale road.

The Simple Journey is to the left; the Less Simple straight on. Disposing first of the Less Simple and continuing up the valley by the side of the stream, when you are two fields from the farm buildings of

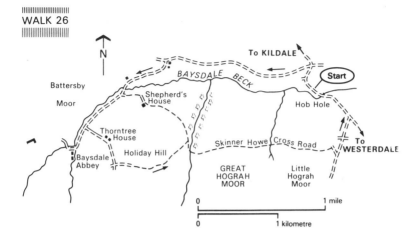

Baysdale Abbey, you will see on the left the track to Thorntree House beyond which is a forest track sloping uphill through the trees. Follow this until, emerging on to the moor, you see a cairn in front of you on the top of Holiday Hill. Go to it. There should be a path but you probably will not find it. Views from the top include the Captain Cook monument on Easby Moor; the tip of Roseberry Topping beyond it; over to the east, a peep into Eskdale. Continuing in the same direction, make for the top trees beside Great Hograh Beck, going through heather until, nearing the trees, you pass some shooting butts. Keep descending towards the trees until you pick up the clear but narrow path coming from Shepherd's House. Turn right.

Those choosing the more straightforward track will walk up the road to Shepherd's House, taking the track to the left of it through the woods to the open moor, continuing forward on the clear path through the heather rounding Holiday Hill. This is Skinner Howe Cross Road which leads to a delightful bridge over Great Hograh Beck, which tumbles over rocks and is tree-lined between here and Baysdale Beck.

The two routes have now converged. Ahead, the narrow track through heather on the rocky Great Hograh Moor is indicated by a succession of stone cairns. It crosses the infant Little Hograh Beck to the moor of the same name, bears slightly to the right, at which point the village of Westerdale comes into sight. Behind the village is Tor Hill, beyond which is the road (to Ralph Crosses) on the Rigg on Westerdale Moor which divides the two arms of the dale.

Soon you will reach another small road with a big name, John Breckon Road, now tarred, which to the right leads to the farms of the upper dale, but turn left to join the slightly wider road from Castleton to Hob Hole. A short downhill walk brings you to the footbridge over Baysdale Beck from which you set out earlier in the day.

83

Walk 27   Danby Beacon

6¼ miles (10 km)

Today's objective offers probably the best all round viewpoint in the National Park north of the river Esk. Although it is easily reached by motor car it is situated in good walking country, worth combining with a visit to the lovely riverside village of Lealholm, the chosen point of embarkation.

Lealholm can be reached from the Whitby/Guisborough road, *via* Stonegate, or locally, by side roads from Danby or Glaisdale. A roomy car park and public toilets are provided near the village green by the river.

Explore the village before setting out. A bridge and stepping stones cross the wide, rippling river. On the south side are picnic areas, an inn and a tea room; on the north, a war memorial and an Edwardian drinking fountain (not in use when last visited) with an old-fashioned substantial iron drinking cup still firmly chained to the stone work.

The walk has been devised to include the trim village of Houlsyke, but to avoid tarmac roads as much as possible. Those who do not wish to follow the detailed field route could take the low road out of Lealholm, picking up the trail at Houlsyke; or if you would prefer a high level road, missing that village, take the uphill road from the car park, passing the 'suburb' of Lealholm Side and, turning left at the road junction above, bear left at the next fork, keeping to the tarmac road for about a mile and a half, and looking out for the white post on the right opposite the gated road coming up from Houlsyke. Turn right and follow the route as detailed below.

Field walkers turn uphill from the car park, cross over the railway and turn left immediately. Pass the station, taking the first gate on the right to go gently uphill on a green track through bracken, to the left of a deep gill. Where the path turns sharply right to go down to the stream, follow it for about 100 yards then fork to the left, going through a gate into a field. Go forward half-right from the apparent track to a gap in the hedge opposite. Skirt the next field on a course parallel to the ravine, keeping a hedge on your right; climb over a stile on the right, 10 yards before the corner (when last visited the stile consisted of two stones and a fence) into a pasture. Bear left, with a hedge now on your left. Pass through three fields, using stone step stiles, partly or completely broken down, in the left-hand corner of each field. Cross the last field to the middle of Park Head Wood, climbing over a fence 20 yards from the field corner. A tree and an

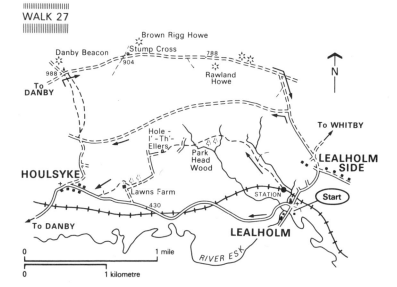

Brown Rigg Howe
Danby Beacon
Stump Cross
788
Rawland Howe
988
904
To DANBY
N
Hole - I' - Th' - Ellers
To WHITBY
Park Head Wood
HOULSYKE
LEALHOLM SIDE
Lawns Farm
STATION
Start
430
To DANBY
LEALHOLM
0   1 mile
RIVER ESK
0   1 kilometre

old notice board mark the spot. Bear right within the wood, cutting off a projecting corner. The right of way is along the upper, right-hand edge of the wood between fences. At the far end of the long field on the right, pass over a small beck on a cart track and bear right to cross the field beyond to a gateway (the top one of four in the opposite hedge). Turn to the left on a cart track on the other side but only for a few yards because the direction of the path is towards the farm on the hillside. Bear right, skirting some boggy ground and going slightly uphill, passing through a gap in the wall and a gate to walk in front of the farmhouse, 'Hole-i'-th'-Ellers,' now disused.

Just beyond and behind the farm is a gate through which pass, keeping in the line of march by the side of a wall on the right, turning left at the other side of a gate in the next wall. A track leads down to a gate on the right of an old farm building. Go through it and turn right past the end of a wall, which is now kept on the right. Make for the trees and, at the back of Lawns Farm, go straight forward to a gate and straight on to another gate on the left. Go through it and cross a field diagonally to the road. Turn right.

We are now walking on ground which was covered by Lake Eskdale at the time of the melting of the glaciers (see also Walk 22). To the left are, first Great Fryup Dale, then Little Fryup Dale, separated by Heads. Soon Houlsyke appears — small and neat. Half-way through the village turn acutely right on a narrow tarmac road where a road sign shows the gradient to be one in four. Keep going uphill, passing a road on the right (to Hollins Farm); pass through a gate and cross another narrow road — the suggested joining point at

85

the end of paragraph four on the previous page.

A white post across the road is at the start of a 'county road' across the moor — a track which is sometimes double, sometimes single, sometimes invisible! But the tall wooden post, with a cross post near the top at the Beacon is soon in sight, giving a clear direction. If in mist, use the line of shooting butts as a general guide.

From Danby Beacon the course of the river Esk from west to east can be traced, together with the valleys of its tributaries, notably Great and Little Fryup Dales comprehensively viewed from this point. The distinctive Easby Moor is away to the west but weather conditions would have to be particularly clear to see the Captain Cook monument on its top. In the northwest, peeping over the line of Danby Low Moor, is Freebrough Hill; it is only 821 feet high but its conical shape is well known to motorists making for Whitby from Teesside, as is also the stretch of water seen to the north of the Beacon, two miles away — Scaling Dam.

Do not be deterred by the mileage shown on the guide post to Lealholm (unfit for motors); for 3¾ read 2¾, at any rate by the direct route, which it is proposed to take, and you will be there in no time! (Or maybe three quarters of an hour). The track is a delight to follow, particularly when the heather is in bloom. After half a mile look to the left for Stump Cross, two stones standing on the old stump, which lies between a cross track junction and Brown Rigg Howe. Before reaching Rawland Howe on the right you will see beyond it, first, Lealholm Side, then, lower down, Lealholm.

Take the right fork, further on, and join the tarmac road which may have been chosen by some on the outward trail. Join the main road where a sign shows Ugthorpe and Whitby to the left, Lealholm and Rosedale to the right. Go downhill past Lealholm Side to the place of departure.

For those seeking serenity in a secluded upland dale followed by some fine views from a prominent point, rocky, among woodlands, here is a tailor-made walk. It may be reduced by a mile if the car driver is willing to go on to the junction before Sleddale Farm on a road which is sometimes rough, sometimes smooth.

On the road between Commondale and Kildale there is a cross road going south-east to Westerdale and north-west to Guisborough. Take the Guisborough road which, although marked 'Unsuitable for Motors', is quite suitable as far as the beginning of the walk. There is a gate to open and close and a sight of the tip of Roseberry Topping as you drive over Brown Hill on this Percy Cross Rigg road. Leave the car at the junction of the Sleddale road on the right, or go gently along it by car for half a mile if you wish.

Do not go down to the farm but walk on the track bearing to the left, going steadily uphill—a sandy, moorland road, good to walk upon. Below, the farm nestles among green fields in the valley bottom, surrounded by heather and bracken moors. The track continues along Codhill Heights making for the mature trees on the left of the younger forest area. It forks and rejoins before reaching a gate in the wall ahead. Look to the right of it for a smaller gate and stile giving access to the wood. On the gate is the acorn sign (the Cleveland Way skirts the fields round Codhill Farm—Highcliffe Farm on the 1:50,000 map—seen below; we shall stay with it until about to leave the forest).

Keep to the well-used, single track, going forward at the lower edge of the wood, which turns to the right opposite another small gate. Cross a wide forest ride and a hundred yards further on the scene opens out. Climb to the top of the Nab which is on the right.

Below is Guisborough, old and new—a really comprehensive picture of its development with the growth of Teesside which can be seen to the north; in clear conditions the Tees and the sea are also in sight. Below left is Hutton Lowcross; further left, the tip of Roseberry Topping; still further left, the Captain Cook monument on Easby Moor.

The route is now due east along the single worn track on the edge of the crag through the forest, with views on the left. Turn left on joining the wide forest ride, turning right off it after a quarter of a mile, where the road dips, on a heather path through a wide cut in the trees to a small gate and a stile. Here is the head of Sleddale.

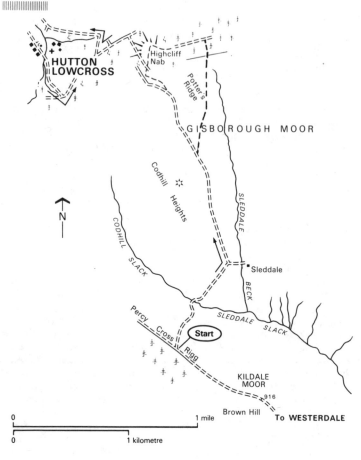

Now follow the Land Rover trail to the right, rejoin the outward track half a mile away and turn left for home.

An alternative walk to the Nab of two miles through the forest may be made from the top end of Hutton Lowcross — a fine residential village. Follow the direction of the arrows shown on the map above.

Walk 29
6½ miles (10.5 km)

The Captain Cook Monument and Roseberry Topping

In some of the most dramatic parts of the National Park, today's journey makes an ideal walk. All the tracks are well marked, if sometimes muddy, and there is something of everything — good shapes, steep cliffs, forest tracks, pastoral valleys and heather moors.

The most accessible start point for the simple climb of Roseberry Topping — 1051 feet above sea level but looking higher because of its conical shape — is the lane just south of the village of Newton-under-Roseberry, which is a little over a mile north of Great Ayton. This is the point used by the White Rose walkers as the beginning of the 34 or 40 mile journey along the tops to the White Horse at Kilburn, starting 336 feet above sea level. Several tracks go up from the wood at the end of the lane, the easiest gradient being found on the wide left hand route over Roseberry Common. The views of the Cleveland Plain from the rocky top are splendid, the patchwork quilt effect being particularly marked in the fields at harvest time when, in late August, the moorland heather should also be at its best.

The start point for the whole round trip now proposed is, however, to be Gribdale Gate where there is accommodation for many cars. To reach it take the road towards Little Ayton out of Great Ayton at the outskirts of which turn left for the railway station, continuing forward uphill as far as the cattle grid at the top, 750 feet above sea level. Park at either side of the cattle grid, near which is a notice board bearing a topographical record of the district.

The Captain Cook monument will be seen to the south. Go through a gate, on which is an acorn sign denoting the Cleveland Way, on to a forest track leading straight up to the monument. The uphill effort will be rewarded at the top by a fine sight to the south of the Lyke Wake 'bumps' of Hasty Bank, Cold Moor, Cringle Moor and beyond. Captain Cook spent his youth at Easby, down below, and went to school in Great Ayton. The memorial is of 'the celebrated circumnavigator Captain James Cook, FRS, a man in nautical knowledge inferior to none . . .'

From the monument, take the obvious green track through the heather to the corner of the wood where, through a gap in a wall, go through a gate in the fence opposite, marked with an acorn. The monument is on Easby Moor; now we move on to Coate Moor, on a good track with a larch wood on the left. Ahead, slightly to the right, is Kildale in the valley of the river Leven. At a fork in the track, bear to the right, soon entering the larch wood. The track joins a metalled

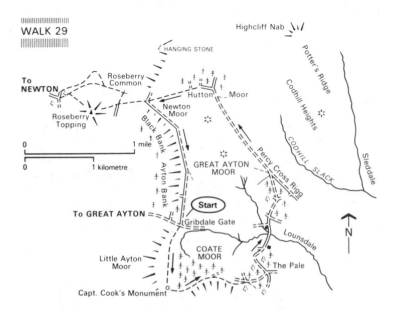

forest road; continue forward, pass through a gate (another acorn) and, 250 yards further on, turn to the left on a tarred by-road, leaving now the Cleveland Way.

The road passes through a mature conifer wood 'Private. Keep Out', downhill into Lounsdale (incorrectly 'Lonsdale' on some maps), beautifully green among the bracken covered hills and forests on the other side. Pass two farms. (One could turn left at the second farm on the road which goes straight back to the car, if one wanted to divide the journey into two). Continuing the original plan, keep straight on; when you reach the forest, join a forest track coming in from the right, bearing left and keeping within the forest boundary. Continue on the main track through the trees, on sand or clay according to season, until you emerge from the forest at a wooden gate and sign reading 'Forestry Commission, Lounsdale'. Now you have reached the Percy Cross Rigg road, tarred up to this point on the right but sandy to the left. Before turning left, have a look round; away to the right are the moors around and beyond Eskdale; immediately below is Codhill Slack, with Sleddale beyond and Potters Ridge between, ending in Highcliff Nab, a viewpoint overlooking Guisborough.

Taking the left turn, along Percy Cross Rigg, on a good walking road among heather, a building can be seen ahead which turns out to be an old air raid shelter or ammunition store. Beyond it there are views of Guisborough on the right, beautifully situated below the hills, and nearer to the forest, now to be seen ahead, a look to the right will reveal Hutton Lowcross in the valley among the trees, looking very much like a Swiss village.

90

Roseberry Topping

At the forest gate there is a notice 'Forestry Commission, Hutton'; turn left when through to the other side, on the road—which can be muddy—on the edge of the forest. Pass a standing stone bearing the date 1834 beside a fire-fighting water reserve (sometimes dry) and go through a small gate on the left. We have returned to the Cleveland Way, as signified by the acorn sign on the other side of the gate. Now follow the single track through the heather on the open moors—first it is Hutton Moor, then Newton Moor—until, breasting the brow, the tip of the Topping comes into sight. Arrive at a corner gate on the edge of Black Bank where you will see there is a sharp drop of 200 feet down to Roseberry Common and a rise of 200 feet to the top; the path is good all the way and you will be well rewarded when you have made the climb.

Return to the corner gate, now bearing right over Newton Moor and Great Ayton Moor both heather covered, but the path is green and good to walk upon. The Monument on Easby Moor can be seen ahead; keep to the side of the wall protecting you from falling over Black Bank and Ayton Bank all the way back to Gribdale Gate.

Wasn't it a grand walk?

Walk 30

7½ miles (12 km)

Greenhow Botton and Bloworth Crossing

This final chapter is a link with the first of these two books, *North York Moors Walks for Motorists* (*West and South*), taking the reader back to the watershed which, in these parts, divides the two volumes, and bringing the walker back to the high country visited on the Lyke Wake Walk, the Cleveland Way, the White Rose Walk and the Rosedale Circuit.

On the way out, an opportunity may be taken to examine the rock strata made clear by the lines of waste heaps from old workings at the top end of Greenhow Botton—*Botton* being a Scandinavian word meaning a rounded valley—and to study the engineering of the old Rosedale Railway, now a right of way, which will be used all the way to Bloworth Crossing, The return will be entirely on the famous moorland road from Kirbymoorside and Rudland Rigg, quite unsuitable for motor vehicles—thank goodness—but used in part by long distance walkers. Surfaces are most suitable for walking on, dry foot, and the route is so simple as to make the mileage seem much less.

Ingleby Greenhow is one of the many lovely villages beautifully situated below the escarpment of the Cleveland Hills near Stokesley. Motoring towards it from any direction is a pleasure; from Helmsley through Bilsdale; from Thirsk, turning off the Stokesley road at Carlton; or from Stokesley, Great Ayton or Kildale. A quarter of a mile out of the village on the road to Battersby and Kildale, take the turning to Bank Foot, parking the car where the road opens out before reaching the farm. Here you will see a sign 'Footpath to Incline' and another 'No admittance to unauthorized vehicles'. Following both instructions on the good surface of the old ironstone railway track, opportunity may be taken to step out and, at the same time, to take stock of the surroundings.

On the immediate right are the grounds of Ingleby Manor, former home of the Sidney family—Lords De L'isle and Dudley; in the middle distance a little knoll, How Hill; and in the background, those famous 'Lyke Wake bumps': Hasty Bank, Cold Moor and Cringle Moor. The valley ahead is Greenhow Botton scooped out and typically glacial, with its stream named on some Ordnance Survey maps 'Ingleby Beck' but on others, 'Eller Beck'—take your choice. At the head of the valley, just over the top and out of sight, is the highest point on the North York Moors, 1491 feet above sea level, on Round Hill at Botton Head, The discerning reader may notice this is two feet higher than is recorded in the first volume, but is in line with the last issue on the 1 inch OS map. Is this difference

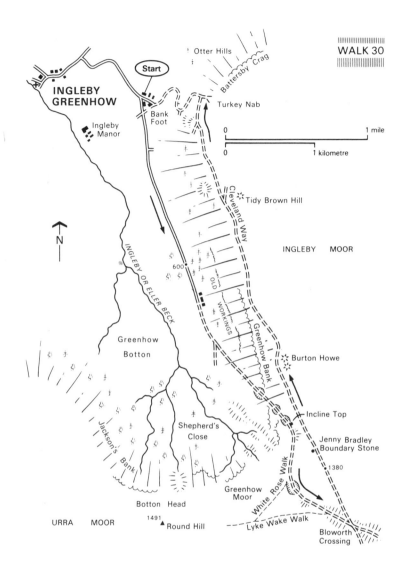

INGLEBY GREENHOW

Ingleby Manor

Start

Bank Foot

Otter Hills

Battersby Crag

Turkey Nab

0   1 mile

0   1 kilometre

Tidy Brown Hill

Cleveland Way

INGLEBY   MOOR

N

INGLEBY OR ELLER BECK

600

OLD WORKINGS

Greenhow Bank

Burton Howe

Greenhow Botton

Jackson's Bank

Shepherd's Close

Incline Top

Jenny Bradley Boundary Stone

1380

Greenhow Moor

White Rose Walk

Botton Head

URRA   MOOR

1491 ▲ Round Hill

Lyke Wake Walk

Bloworth Crossing

the height of the triangulation pillar? The track ahead will cut through the rocky Greenhow Bank on Greenhow Moor. The moor on our immediate left, above the conifers, is Ingleby Moor.

Pass four ex-railway cottages, a roundabout for 'authorized' vehicles, go through a gate placed across the road, and start the steady climb from 650 feet above sea level to 1375 at Incline Top. A forest road goes straight on which can be seen to curve round the head of the valley through young plantations. Pausing for breath half way up the incline, look to the right front and one may see where contractors have taken mains for natural gas, utilizing an existing run-way from old mines. Red markers indicate the position of the pipes.

The track goes through three cuttings and passes what remains of the old winding house at Incline Top, after which the going is pretty level. White Rose walkers join our route here but not for long because at the next cutting, where there is a stile to be climbed, the long distance walkers turn off to the right but we keep to the old line, soon joining Lyke Wake walkers as far as Bloworth Crossing where there is a gate across the railway track.

This is a famous place: the Lyke Wake Walk goes straight on, keeping to the railway for some distance; the road to the right is to Rudland Rigg; to the left is the turning taken by Cleveland Wayfarers; and so do we.

The first item of interest is the Jenny Bradley stone, marking the boundary of the Ingleby Estate; on the right, further on, is Burton Howe (according to OS map, but 'Botton Howe', which seems right, according to Bill Cowley in his book *The Cleveland Way*). The path returns to the moor edge where rocky outcrops could provide a playground and shelter if needed; a little further north 20 yards from the road, on the right, is another stone, well marked and with a hollow top, similar to Ralph Cross East's hollow, in which alms were formerly left for the traveller. These two stones are fully described by Bill Cowley.

Pass a low stone on the left, marked Greenhow Road, and when you reach two adjoining gates on the right, at Tidy Brown Hill, leave the route taken by walkers on the Cleveland Way and White Rose Walk by continuing straight forward on the 'main' road. An acorn on the gate denotes the turning for the long distance walkers but there should also be a 'Cleveland Way' sign.

Our road soon loses height until, at a corner, where there is an old railway parcels van, a fine scene reveals itself: the Captain Cook monument and Roseberry Topping will have been seen from time to time on the way, but now they make a splendid backcloth to the vale of the river Leven, which flows below Easby Moor on which the Cook monument stands. The village below is Battersby, the terrace to the left being at Battersby junction. Away to the right, below the nab, is Kildale. This viewpoint is known as Turkey Nab, but, strangely enough, it is not named on Ordnance Survey maps.

Now wind your way downhill and you will soon be back at Bank Foot.

Some Useful Addresses and Publications

For complaints about obstruction of rights of way:
North York Moors National Park Office, The Old Vicarage, Bondgate, Helmsley, N.Yorks YO6 5BP.

National Park Information

North York Moors National Park Information Service, The Old Vicarage, Bondgate, Helmsley, N. Yorks YO6 5BP.

The National Park Planning Committee have established nature reserves and farm trails in the Park. Within the area covered by this book are Ravenscar Nature Trail and May Beck Farm Trail. All trail guides are available by post from the above address.

Much more information is obtainable from the National Park Information Centres at Sutton Bank, Pickering Station, and Danby, well worth a visit.

National Park Warden

Mr R. Bell, Sutherland Cottage, Cropton, Pickering, N. Yorkshire.

Forestry

District Officer, Forestry Commission, 42 Eastgate, Pickering. N. Yorkshire.

Visit the Forestry Information Centre at Low Dalby on the Forest Ride, north of Thornton-le-Dale.

Nature Reserves

There are eight within the Park. Nature Trail guides may be obtained from: The Yorkshire Naturalists' Trust, 20 Castlegate, York, YO1 1RP.

Accommodation

The Yorkshire and Humberside Tourist Board, 312 Tadcaster Road, York (Tel. York 67961) publishes a guide, which includes an accommodation list covering the whole of Yorkshire.

The North York Moors National Park Information Service (address above) publishes a register of accommodation for the area. It also supplies a leaflet on Youth Hostels, caravan and camp sites. Local guides (which contain accommodation advertisements) are obtainable from the following local councils:

Langbaurgh Borough Council, Albion Terrace, Saltburn, Cleveland. Tel Saltburn 2013.

Hambleton District Council, The Old Vicarage, Northallerton DL7 8DL. Tel Northallerton 6101.

Ryedale District Council, Ryedale House, Malton, N. Yorkshire. Tel Malton 4941.

Scarborough Borough Council, Information Centre, St Nicholas Cliff, Scarborough, N. Yorkshire. Tel. Scarborough 72261.

Whitby—Publicity Officer, The Spa, Whitby,. N. Yorkshire.

Official Guides

National Park Guide No 4: North York Moors. Arthur Raistrick (ed.). 3rd edn. 1977. H.M.S.O. for the Countryside Commission. (The official guide provides an introduction to most aspects of study.)

North Yorkshire Forest Guide. 1972. H.M.S.O.

Other Publications

Yorkshire Field Studies. (Series 1). G.E. Bell, 1967. (Covers 51 field excursions of which five are in and around the Park.) University of Leeds, Institute of Education.

Abbeys of Yorkshire. K. Wilson. 1969. Dalesman Publishing Co. Ltd

The Naturalists' Yorkshire. Yorkshire Naturalists' Union. 1971.

Railways in Cleveland. K. Hoole, 1972. Dalesman Publishing Co. Ltd.

Whitby and Pickering Railway. D. Joy. 1971. Dalesman Publishing Co. Ltd.

Exploring the North York Moors, Malcolm Boyes. 1976. Dalesman Publishing Co. Ltd.

The North York Moors—an Introduction. Stanhope White. 1979. Dalesman Publishing Co. Ltd.

Long Distance Walks

Lyke Wake Walk. Bill Cowley. 1959. Dalesman Publishing Co. Ltd. Forty miles across the North Yorkshire Moors.

The Cleveland Way. Bill Cowley. 1969. Dalesman Publishing Co. Ltd. Yorkshire Moors and Coast Footpath.

The White Rose Walk. Geoffrey White. 1973. Dalesman Publishing Co. Ltd. From Roseberry Topping to the White Horse.

The Crosses Walk. Malcolm Boyes. 1974. Dalesman Publishing Co. Ltd. 53 miles over the North York Moors.

A Guide to the Cleveland Way and Missing Link. Malcolm Boyes. 1977. Constable & Co.

The Rosedale Circuit. 37 miles. Details of route from The Rosedale Circuit Secretary, British Aerospace Aircraft Group, Blackburn Welfare Society, Rambling Club Section, Brough, N. Humberside HU15 1EQ. Send stamped addressed envelope.

The Forest Walk, Reasty to Allerston. Details of route from The Walk Secretary, Forestry Commission, 42 Eastgate, Pickering, N. Yorkshire. Send stamped addressed envelope.

The Samaritan Way. 40-mile circular from Guisborough, Send s.a.e. To R.T. Pinkney, 11 Pine Road, North Ormesby, Middlesbrough.

The Wydale Walk. 20 miles. Wydale Hall, York Diocesan House, to Robin Hood's Bay. Send s.a.e. to Rev. L.S. Rivett, B.A., Warden, Wydale Hall, Brompton-by-Sawdon, Scarborough, N. Yorkshire YO13 9DG.

The Bilsdale Circuit, Michael Teanby, 30 miles around Bilsdale. Published by the Dalesman Publishing Co. Ltd.

STOCKTON-BILLINGHAM
LIBRARY
TECHNICAL COLLEGE